IAN ALLAN
TRANSPORT LIBRARY

Birmingham Corporation Transport 1904-1939

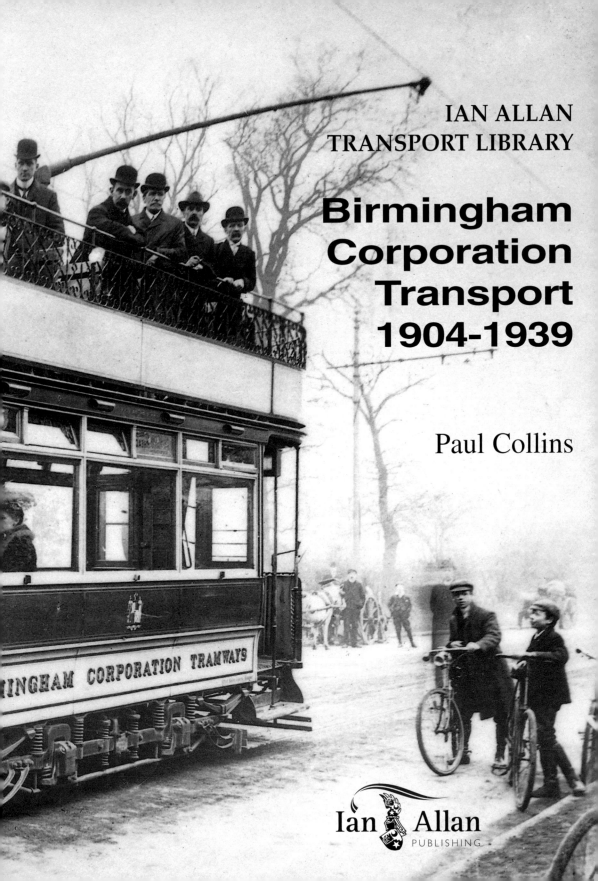

IAN ALLAN
TRANSPORT LIBRARY

Birmingham Corporation Transport 1904-1939

Paul Collins

Ian Allan
PUBLISHING

Contents

Front cover: By the 1930s Birmingham Corporation had become a tram, bus and trolleybus operator, and one of the best places to see all three in action was in Digbeth. At the junction with Rea Street, trolleybuses are city-bound and trams head off into the suburbs, whilst the rest of the traffic does its best to avoid them – with varying degrees of success. *Birmingham Post & Mail*

Back cover, top: Like other tramway operators, Birmingham Corporation experimented with modern tramcar designs in the late 1920s. Car No 842 had an all-metal body by Short Bros of Rochester, and seated 63 in unparalleled luxury. Seen here on the loop at Rednal terminus in December 1929, 842 was destined to be the Corporation's penultimate new tramcar. *IAL*

Back cover, bottom: Car 842's lines make quite a contrast in modernity when compared with Corporation bus 352, an AEC Regent, which was one of 30 also delivered in 1929. Nonetheless, for bus passengers it represented a great step forward, as the vehicles were the first to feature enclosed staircases and comfortable upholstered seating. *IAL*

Half title: A front three-quarter view of Corporation trolleybus No 6 outside Washwood Heath depot, showing its very tramcar-like appearance. The trolleybuses used the single tramway overhead wire, and made a current return through a metal skate, positioned in one of the tram rails which was dragged along behind the vehicle. *National Motor Museum*

Title: It was Civic Pride, cycles, and the only lady downstairs for the opening of Birmingham Corporation's new route to Erdington on 22 April 1907. This was shortly after the expiry of the BCT Co leases, which allowed the Corporation massively to expand its tramway operations. *Tramway & Light Railway World/IAL*

Right: Amber Rays Family Ale, Lewis's Splendid Hats and a 4d Haircut were amongst the delights awaiting passengers who alighted from this CBT cable car outside the entrance to the Great Western Arcade in Colmore Row. *Whybrow Collection*

First published 1999

ISBN 0 7110 2627 0

Published by Ian Allan Publishing

an imprint of Ian Allan Publishing Ltd, Terminal House, Shepperton, Surrey TW17 8AS.
Printed by Ian Allan Printing Ltd, Riverdene Business Park, Hersham, Surrey KT12 4RG.

Code: 9912/B

Introduction

THE GROWTH OF THE CITY

'Birmingham' is derived from Anglo-Saxon dialect, the area now occupied by the city once being the ham or 'home' of the 'followers' or ing of Berm: the 'Bermings'' home. A 'Bermingeham' was recorded in Doomsday Book in 1084, with a population of around 60, and a combined land and property value of just 20s. Around 1166, Henry I granted Peter de Bermingham, Lord of the Manor, the right to hold a weekly market. The de Bermingham family reigned over the town until 1529, when the young Edward de Bermingham was deprived of the Manor by his guardian by virtue of his involvement in a robbery from one of his tenants.

Surveying England in 1538 for Henry VIII, John Leland recorded the foundations of Birmingham's industrial history, with smiths, cutlers, and a great many nailers seen at work. During the Civil War the town sided with the Parliamentary cause, with much of its involvement centred around Aston Hall, where Charles I rested en route to the Battle of Edgehill in 1642, and which was besieged for three days in 1643. Following the Civil War there was a great diversification in the town's industries; sword- and pike-making being added to its output. Towards the end of the 17th century the gun trade became established, and during the Napoleonic Wars 1.75 million muskets were produced in Birmingham for the British Army.

The town's prosperity increased throughout the 18th century, founded upon the manufacture of metal 'toys': precision-made objects, such as shoe and hat buckles, which were produced in vast quantities. Birmingham's most celebrated toy manufacturer was Matthew Boulton, to whose Soho Foundry in Smethwick came James Watt, the improver of the steam engine. Together they produced the machines which powered the Industrial Revolution and founded the nation's wealth. By 1800 Birmingham's population had increased to 70,000, and new industries, such as the manufacture of pens and jewellery, had become established.

Industrial activity, fostered by the coming of the canals, from 2 November 1769, and railways, from 4 July 1838, brought increased prosperity, and enabled the Town Council to initiate a series of 'improvements' which led to the setting out of the Victorian City seen today. Birmingham became a Parliamentary Borough in 1832, and was incorporated as a Borough on 1 November 1838. From that date the enterprise of the Town Council, most notably after Joseph Chamberlain entered public life in 1869, was remarkable. This was formally recognised on 14 January 1889, when Queen Victoria raised the town to the status of a City, and again in

Right: Birmingham has its origins in Saxon times, with forest clearing around the River Rea. For many centuries the town was centred around Digbeth and Deritend, with St Martin's Church at its hub. This is Birmingham in 1731, by which time New Street and Moor Street were amongst the now familiar thoroughfares established. *Author's Collection*

1896, when Her Majesty granted the title of Lord Mayor to its Chief Magistrate.

Throughout this period the town/city grew vastly in population, but little in size. There was also an anomalous situation which saw adjoining districts such as Harborne and Saltley included in the Birmingham Parliamentary Borough, but excluded from the Council's control. Moves to correct this were made in 1890, and in 1891 the City was increased by the addition of Saltley and Little Bromwich (from Warwickshire), Harborne (from Staffordshire), and Balsall Heath (from Worcestershire), which increased it from 8,340 to 12,365 acres. Another addition was made on 9 November 1909, when the Parish of Quinton was annexed from Warley, increasing the City to 13,477 acres, with a population of 526,000.

Further expansion was inevitable, and a Greater Birmingham Scheme was promoted to bring this about. After securing Parliamentary approval and Royal Assent, this Scheme took effect from 9 November 1911, and was one of the biggest boundary revisions in British history. Aston Manor, Erdington UDC, Handsworth UDC, King's Norton & Northfield UDC, plus Yardley RDC were added to the City, increasing its area to 43,537 acres, and the population to 867,000. Some of these new districts were very populous and prosperous. King's Norton & Northfield UDC was one of the largest urban districts in England. It included Moseley, King's Heath, Selly Oak, Stirchley and Bournville, and its population had risen dramatically from 28,300 in 1891 to over 70,000 by 1904.

Birmingham has expanded three more times since 1911, with part of Perry Barr UDC being added on 1 April 1928, bringing the City up to 46,487 acres, part of Solihull, and portions of the parishes of Castle Bromwich, Minworth and Sheldon being added on 1 April 1931, making the City 51,147 acres; finally, the addition of Sutton Coldfield on 1 April 1974 brought the total acreage up to 65,125.

Many notable people have Birmingham connections, including the members of the town's Lunar Society: John Baskerville, Matthew Boulton, William Murdoch, Joseph Priestley and James Watt, the politicians Joseph and Neville Chamberlain, and the comedians Sid Field and Tony Hancock.

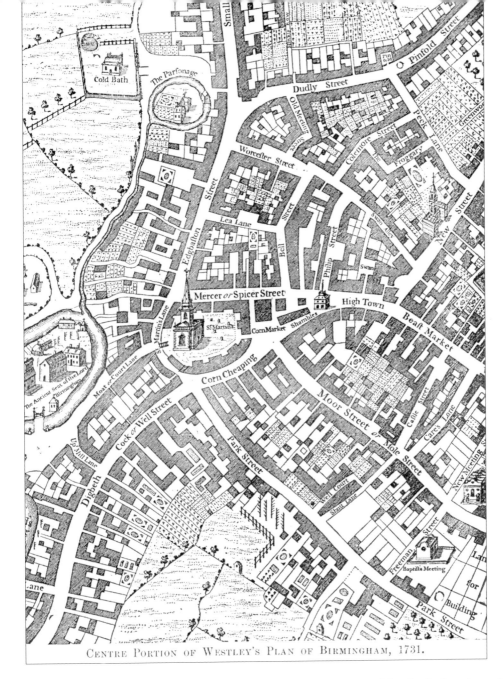

CENTRE PORTION OF WESTLEY'S PLAN OF BIRMINGHAM, 1731.

Following World War 2, Birmingham became notorious for its wholesale redevelopment, which began with the widening of Digbeth in 1954/5, and continued with the building of the Inner Ring Road (1959-71) and Bull Ring Shopping Centre (1964), the rebuilding of New Street station (1963-7), and the Newtown, Nechells, Lee Brook, Highgate and Ladywood housing schemes, all of which were symbolised by one building, a cylindrical office block called the Rotunda (1965). Over 30 years on, the Rotunda is a listed building and the Bull Ring area faces imminent redevelopment. The Council has also finally woken up to its heritage, with the enhancement of the Jewellery Quarter and the upgrading of the canals through the City.

Writing in the first edition of his history of Birmingham in 1780, William Hutton observed that: 'Birmingham may be considered as one vast and modern edifice, of which the ancient materials make but a very small part; the extensive new seems to surround the minute old, as if to protect it.' The intervening 220 years seem to have made very little difference.

1. Public Transport in the Pre-Corporation Days

ORIGINS

Public transport in Birmingham has a history that may go back 300 years. Stagecoaches may have been operating there since the late 17th century, but evidence of the earliest known stagecoach service, to London on 24 May 1731, comes from a surviving handbill. There was also one hackney coach operating in the town in 1775, but by 1819 this number had increased to at least 30. Birmingham's first omnibus was operated by John Smith of The Malt Shovel, Smallbrook Street, and run from The Swan, Snow Hill, to the Bristol Road tollgate from 5 May 1834. It used two horses, seated 12 inside, and had a flat fare of 6d (2½p). By 1837 competing operators were offering services to Bromsgrove, Dudley, Kidderminster, Stourbridge, Wednesbury, West Bromwich and Wolverhampton, amongst others.

EARLY TRAMWAY PROPOSALS

Birmingham did not escape the attention of the tramway pioneer George Francis Train, and on 7 August 1860 he reached an agreement with the Town Council to construct a tramway from New Street to Ivy Bush via Paradise Street, Broad Street and Five Ways. The scheme was not proceeded with as the Birmingham Improvement Act, 1861, gave the

Council powers to build its own tramways, and to 'permit the same to be used by waggon cart, carriage or vehicle adopted to use the same, and drawn by Animal Power'. It was therefore felt unnecessary to have to delegate these powers to a private individual. Nonetheless, as late as 1862, Train was still insisting that he had the capital and workforce available to construct the line.

In the years that followed, the number of omnibus operators grew, and in May 1869 William and Daniel Busby of Liverpool formed the Birmingham Omnibus Co to merge the interests of 10 operators and pool approximately 40 vehicles. As a result, on 2 June 1869 a number of horse omnibus routes were introduced. The Busbys' interests also went beyond omnibuses, and by November 1869 they were proposing a tramway scheme, and intending to promote a 'Birmingham Tramways Co'. A similar tramway scheme was promoted at around this time by the Birmingham Street

Below: New Street c1900, with the General Post Office on the right. All of the vehicles in view are horse-drawn, including the omnibuses. The one waiting by the statue of Sir Robert Peel is bound for Harborne, as someone tends to a gas lamp atop a pair of steps. *Author's Collection*

Tramways Co, and the Birmingham & Staffordshire Tramways Co published plans for a line to Dudley Port.

These proposals automatically involved the Town Council, and early in 1870 its Public Works Committee reported that it had examined the bills then before Parliament from the Birmingham & Staffordshire Tramways, the Birmingham Street Tramways and the Birmingham Tramways, each of which was seeking exclusive rights to lay tracks in certain streets. After negotiation it was resolved that the Council should retain its right to lay the tracks and lease these out to the tramway companies. The two latter-named concerns also merged to form Birmingham Suburban Tramways.

Meanwhile, many omnibuses continued to ply the streets, and in August 1869 Birmingham Council's Watch Committee responded to complaints regarding the inconvenience caused by the large omnibus traffic in High Street. Arrangements were made to ensure that they did not stand there longer than was necessary to pick up passengers. The Council also paid the Governors of King Edward's School £1 per annum for use of land in Albert Street as a waiting place — the town's first 'bus stop.

THE TRAMWAYS ACT AND ITS CONSEQUENCES

The Tramways Act became law on 9 August 1870, and gave councils the power to construct tramways by a Provisional Order. This was adopted by Birmingham Council, its estimates showing that each yard of single-line tramway, including granite sett paving, would cost £2 10s per yard to construct. Not that any tramways had actually been constructed, the various schemes being held up by 'negotiations' with the Council, which was seeking to protect its interests. In an attempt to get things moving, the Birmingham & District Tramways Co Ltd was formed on 29 July 1871, to take over all three tramway schemes proposed for the town, plus the Birmingham Omnibus Co. The move was successful, for on Whit Monday (20 May) 1872, the Birmingham & District Tramways Co Ltd opened a standard-gauge horse tramway from Dudley Port to the Birmingham boundary via West Bromwich and Handsworth.

Now at least there was a tramway *to* Birmingham, if not exactly *in* it, but this did not prevent the Council's Public Works Committee from producing its first by-laws for the regulation of tramway operation in 1873. These stipulated a minimum speed of 6mph, and a maximum of 8mph, with at least a 100ft headway to be left between tramcars in operation. Special 'carriages' for the 'labouring classes' were to be run between 5.30 and 6.30am and 5.30 and 6.30pm, and the seating capacity was to be shown on each vehicle, based upon an allowance of 16in per person. These by-laws were occasioned by the impending opening of a standard-gauge horse tramway built by Birmingham Corporation between Monmouth Street and Hockley, where it connected with the Birmingham & District Tramways Co Ltd horse tramway to West Bromwich and Dudley Port. This opened formally on 6 September 1873 and was operated by the same company. The *Birmingham Post* described the cars on the opening day: 'The carriages are light, commodious, comfortable and convenient. They measure 12ft 9in by 6ft wide inside and seat

Below: The symbol of Birmingham's emerging civic pride was the new Council House, opened in 1878, and the Art Gallery, opened in 1885. They are seen here c1900 with a CBT omnibus and two Hansom cabs, developed by the same person who designed Birmingham's Town Hall. *Author's Collection*

Below: Both the shovel hanging up in the cab and the pair of ash pits behind the trailer serve as reminders of just how arduous a job it was to drive a steam tram. None the less, the driver of this CBT tram bound for Witton seems decidedly more cheerful than his rather dour conductor. *Author's Collection*

Bottom: Birmingham & District Tramways Co car No 17 was built at Saltley by the Metropolitan Railway & Wagon Co in 1873 and seated 36 (18/18). Unlike the later tramways in the City, the B&DT was a standard-gauge system. *Whitcombe Collection, Science Museum*

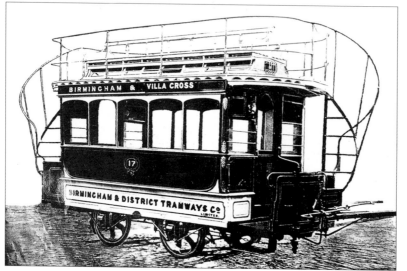

Above: Lately reinstated, with an overdue memorial to comic Tony Hancock, Old Square was once the focal point for steam tram operation in Birmingham. In 1903 CBT locomotive No 11 worked a trailer to Saltley, while Birmingham & Aston Tramways loco No 1 worked to Aston in the shadow of Newbury's department store, which preceded Lewis's on that site. *Author's Collection*

18 inside and 18 outside. They are fitted with two paraffin lamps and were constructed by the Metropolitan Carriage & Wagon Co of Saltley.' The fares were 2d to Hunters Lane, 3d to Villa Cross, and 1d per mile beyond. The same fare was charged for travel inside or out. Public services may not have started until 11 September. The lease payable to the Corporation was £910 per annum.

Things were rarely static for long in the development of public transport in Birmingham, and on 24 May 1876 the Birmingham Tramways & Omnibus Co Ltd was formed to take over the Birmingham & District Tramways Co and to amalgamate it with William Mayner's omnibus business in Handsworth. Less than a month later, on 17 June, a second standard-gauge horse tramway opened. This started from the first line in Monmouth Street and ran via Ann Street (now Colmore Row), Paradise Street and Suffolk Street to the Bristol Road, and on to Bournbrook. It was double-track to Belgrave Road, and single with passing loops beyond. The Birmingham & District Tramways Co agreed to pay a lease of £1,500 per annum for this and the Hockley line combined.

STEAM AND NARROW GAUGE TRAMWAYS

In 1880 Birmingham Council's Public Works Committee and the Aston Local Board set up a joint committee to examine proposed tramway construction in both areas by the Birmingham & Aston Tramways Co. Powers obtained in the Parliamentary Act would be transferred to the Corporation, which would build the line and lease it to the company for 21 years at £300 per annum, rising to £450 after 14 years.

To this date all tramways constructed in Birmingham had been standard-gauge, but whilst work was in process, the gauge stipulated in the Birmingham & Western District Tramways Order 1881 was changed to 3ft 6in by the Board of Trade, which cited the narrowness of some of the streets in justification. This was then duly adopted as the tramway gauge in Birmingham, and a narrow-groove rail section approved, which did not allow a standard-gauge wheel to run in it.

The next tramway to open, operated by the Birmingham & Aston Tramways Co Ltd, represented a significant development. On 26 December 1882 that company opened a

Above: By the 1890s the Hagley Road was well served by horse omnibus services. The main thoroughfare into the City from the wealthy suburb of Edgbaston, services were as frequent as one every 15min, and, as on this service from Bearwood, used three horses on what is quite a flat route. *Author's Collection*

Left: The well-regimented line of pinafore-dressed schoolgirls outside Newbury's has a wealth of activity to witness in Old Square as an LNWR Collecting Van waits outside Lunts and passengers hurriedly alight from a newly-arrived steam tram. *Whybrow Collection*

Below: Few cities could rival the variety of tramway traction available in Birmingham at the turn of the 20th century, although the fleet number on CBT cable car No 175 is misleading as to the size of this particular undertaking: the cable cars were numbered in sequence with the company's other trams in the City. *Dudley Libraries/Author's Collection*

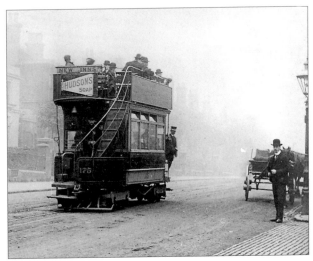

3ft 6in gauge steam tramway from Aston Street to Aston Cross, where the line forked, one half running via Park Road and Witton Lane to Witton, the other reaching Witton via Lichfield Road and Church Road. This was both the City's first narrow-gauge tramway, and the first to be worked by mechanical traction. Permission to use steam traction was only granted after information had been received from Edinburgh, Hanley and Leeds, and a visit made to a steam tramway in Blackburn. In 1885 this tramway was extended from Aston Cross to Salford Bridge, and on by horse omnibus to Erdington.

Two more tramway companies were formed in 1883: the Birmingham Central Tramways Co Ltd, on 24 January, to operate routes in both the north and south of the City, and the Birmingham & Midland Tramways Co Ltd, registered on 22 November. Unfortunately, that year the Council refused to sanction further steam tramways until more experience had been gained on the Aston route. There was gross overcrowding on some cars, especially those travelling from Old Square on Saturdays. Cars built to take 60 regularly had 120 or more persons on board; their brakes were not always in good order, and the crews were reluctant to apply them.

The next development did not involve steam traction. In October 1884 the Public Works Committee received an offer from the Patent Cable Tramways Corporation Ltd to lease the Birmingham Central Tramway Co's lines and convert them to cable operation. The former deposited £15,000 on account as proof of its *bona fides*. Before reaching a decision, the Committee received information from cable tramways in San Francisco, Chicago and Philadelphia, and a visit was made to the cable tramway then running in Highgate, London.

On 11 November 1884 the Birmingham Central Tramways Co Ltd opened a 3ft 6in gauge horse tramway from Old Square to Nechells Park Road (Needham Street) via Great Lister Street, but by this time the Corporation must have begun to sanction steam tramway operation once more, because the same company opened two steam-worked lines before the year's end:

- 25 November — Old Square-Newtown Row-Perry Barr;
- 29 December — Bradford Street-Moseley Road
  (Moseley Village).

In February 1885 the Birmingham & Aston Tramways Co began operation of a steam tramway from Old Square to Gravelly Hill, and Birmingham Central Tramways opened a works in Kyotts Lake Road, Sparkbrook, for the repair and operation of steam trams — an establishment destined to play a key role in the future of all tramways in Birmingham. Later that year this company also opened three more steam tramway lines:

- March — Smithfield-Bradford Street-Stratford Road
  (Showell Green Lane);
- 11 May — Sparkbrook (extended to College Road,
  Sparkhill in June 1900);
- 24 November — Old Square-Saltley via Gosta Green.

That narrow-gauge tramways had established such a hold in the City was demonstrated in 1885. On 30 April, when the Birmingham Tramways & Omnibus Co Ltd's lease of its tramway lines expired, renewal was made contingent upon these being relaid to the 3ft 6in gauge. Equally demonstrative was the Birmingham Central Tramways Co's moving in June of its Smithfield terminus to Station Street, reached via Bromsgrove Street and Hill Street, as was the opening on 6 July of that portion of the Birmingham & Midland Tramways Ltd's 10-mile 3ft 6in gauge steam tramway situated within the City. The full line ran from Lionel Street (Summer Row) to Dudley via Smethwick and Oldbury, with a loop to West Bromwich (Paradise Street) via Spon Lane and Bromford Lane; it opened through to Dudley on 30 August.

On 20 October 1885, a year after its initial offer, the Patent Cable Tramways Corporation Ltd's bid for the Birmingham Central Tramways Co's lines was accepted in part, being confined to the Hockley and Bournbrook lines. The Central company was granted a lease for 21 years, and authorised to work the Cable Corporation's patent. All of the following two years' tramway developments were also by the Birmingham Central Tramways Co. On 1 January 1886 it purchased the Birmingham Tramways & Omnibus Co Ltd's tramway and omnibus undertaking, also leasing all the tramway lines it worked within the City for 21 years.

Left: Once again, use of the fleet number 106 in the CBT fleet belied the fact that there were just 12 of these battery accumulator tramcars working one route to Bournbrook.
Birmingham's first electric trams last ran in May 1901, by which time they were scarred and weakened by acid spills.
Author's Collection

The company also opened two new steam tramways from its new Station Street terminus:

- 16 January — Station Street-Coventry Road-Small Heath;
- 19 July — Station Street-Sherlock Street-Balsall Heath-Moseley;
- 25 October — Wheeler Street.

In 1887 it opened two more:

- 1 February — Extension of the Moseley route to King's Heath;
- 1 June — Engine Inn (Great Hampton Row)-Wheeler Street-Lozells (Aston boundary).

THE FIRST ELECTRIC TRAMWAY

On 24 March 1888 the Birmingham Central Tramways Co reopened the original Monmouth Street-Hockley standard-gauge tramway, relaid to 3ft 6in gauge and equipped for cable operation. This proved successful, and on 20 April 1889 it was extended to the New Inns, Handsworth. For want of knowing what to do with the standard-gauge Bristol Road tramway route, in 1888 the Central company experimented with the use of an accumulator-powered electric locomotive on it. This must have been successful, for in 1889 the tramway was reconstructed to 3ft 6in gauge, and on 1 July

1890 the Bristol Road and Hockley tramway lines were leased to the Birmingham Central Tramways Co for 21 years, including lines in Great Hampton Row and Wheeler Street. Three weeks later, on 24 July, the Bristol Road line reopened, operated by battery-electric cars. These ran to the former horse tramway depot in Dawlish Road; the track along Colmore Row, formerly connecting the two old horse tramways, was not relaid, and thus the routes were no longer connected.

MOVES TOWARDS ELECTRIFICATION

The opening of the South Staffordshire Tramways overhead electric system on 1 January 1893 signalled the way ahead for many tramway operators, and it was not long before similar proposals were being made for Birmingham. In 1894, conversion of the Bristol Road tramway to overhead electric traction was proposed, and in 1895 a similar scheme was proposed for the Nechells route. Others, sensing that when electrification came it would not be done piecemeal, set about forming larger groups of interests. In 1896 there was an amalgamation of several independent omnibus companies to form the Birmingham & District Omnibus Co, done to 'effect a monopoly of the omnibus system in Birmingham', and on 29 September 1896 a new tramway company, with an official sounding name — the City of Birmingham Tramways Co Ltd (CBT) — was formed to take over the assets of the

Above: Overhead electric tramways approached Birmingham from the suburbs and outlying districts. From the northwest the BET-controlled South Staffordshire Tramways Co opened electrified lines through West Bromwich to the Handsworth boundary on 20 December 1902. This view shows a car in High Street, West Bromwich.
Commercial Postcard/Author's Collection

Birmingham Central Tramways Co Ltd. The sense of making such protective moves was soon to be seen.

On 26 October 1896 the British Electric Traction Co Ltd (BET) was formed, to take over horse and steam tramways and electrify them. Well-resourced, BET would prove to be amongst the most predatory of companies, and found a natural stalking-ground in the West Midlands. In 1897 it bought the electrified lines of the South Staffordshire Tramways Co Ltd, taking possession of the company in June 1900. BET's first toehold in Birmingham came when it bought the assets of a bankrupt omnibus company, the Birmingham General Omnibus Co, operating it from 27 September 1899. This had been renamed from the Birmingham & District Omnibus Co in April 1897. Persisting with this, in March 1900 BET ordered new omnibuses for its Birmingham General omnibus operation, and decided to have them painted red.

Meanwhile, on 7 June 1897, negotiations between CBT and Birmingham Corporation over the electrification of the City's tramways using the overhead system broke down, the City Corporation preferring to use the conduit system. Pursuing its own plans, two years later, on 7 March 1899, the Corporation sought Parliamentary powers to work all the tramways within the City upon the expiry of the various leases, and on 1 January 1900, bought the Birmingham Electric Supply Co Ltd for £420,000. Negotiations resumed with CBT, which on 1 May 1900 gained approval to electrify the Bristol Road route with the overhead system. Two months later, on 21 July 1900 the Corporation agreed to purchase the rolling stock, feeder and overhead on the Bristol Road, within the City boundary, from CBT on 1 July 1911, the day after the lease was due to expire.

Up to this point, tramway matters had been dealt with by the City's Public Works Committee, mainly because they all involved roadworks. The pace of change with tramways in the City is reflected in the fact that on 9 November 1900 the Council formed a new Tramways Committee to take over this responsibility.

ELECTRIFICATION AT LAST

In January 1901 BET purchased a large block of shares in the Birmingham & Midland Tramways, and on 1 January 1902 operation of the BET-owned Birmingham General Omnibus Co was placed under the control of this company. The red omnibuses used quickly led to the description 'Midland Red'.

On 14 May 1901 the Suffolk Street-Bournbrook battery-electric route reopened as an overhead electric tramway — the first in the City — operated by CBT. Just over a year later, in June 1902, this company was taken over by BET. A few weeks later, on 30 June, Aston Manor UDC purchased the Birmingham & Aston Tramways Co Ltd, and on 20 December electrification of the BET-owned South Staffordshire Tramways Co's lines reached the Handsworth/West Bromwich boundary at the Woodman Inn.

By the end of 1902, the City of Birmingham was served by electric tramways, but none was under the direct control of the City Corporation, which, in most cases, had been neatly outflanked by the cunning and predatory BET, which had a monopoly of omnibus operation and a near-monopoly of tramway operation in the City.

2. 1903-1910: Formation

Birmingham's Tramways Committee faced a daunting task. It owned a tramway system, but the services were operated by private companies, some with leases running for as long as 20 years. Undaunted, it devised a programme of construction and reconstruction to modernise and electrify routes to eight districts of the City. Priority was given to the tramway between Old Square and the Aston boundary as the lease on this line would be the first to expire, on 31 December 1903. To co-ordinate this work, the Committee sought a General Manager for the Tramways Department, and found an ideal candidate in Alfred Baker, Chief Officer of London County Council Tramways, whose long tenure in the post would see the undertaking through to the late 1920s.

With a first route open, attention turned to work on nine tramways, comprising just over 21 route miles. Attention also turned to negotiating with BET, which leased and ran tramways on behalf of Aston Manor Borough Council, King's Norton & Northfield UDC, the South Staffordshire Tramways (Lessee) Co and the Birmingham & Midland Tramways Co. Agreement was reached to allow the reconstruction of four routes prior to the expiry of leases at the end of 1906; this period also saw the last horse and steam tramcars run in the

City. As a result, at the start of 1907 the Corporation became a major tramway operator, working nine new routes, but a fatal tramway accident that October was a chastening experience for all involved.

New tramways needed tramcars to work them, and in the period in question the Corporation acquired 360 new ones, and experimented with fitting top covers to some of these. New depots were provided too, on the Coventry Road and at Washwood Heath, and others planned, nearly £100,000 being spent on land and buildings for this purpose.

With time against its continued operation of tramways in the City, BET was at least involved in the first use of motor omnibuses in Birmingham. This had been started on 12 April 1904 by the Birmingham Motor Express Co, which had turned itself into BMMO (Birmingham & Midland Motor

Below: Birmingham's first overhead electric tramway was its first electric route to Bournbrook. Electrified and extended to Selly Oak by CBT, this opened on 14 May 1901. In 1903 the company bought eight of these bogie tramcars (Nos 181-8) to work the route from the Brush Electrical Co, where No 181 is seen prior to delivery.
Brush Electrical Co/National Tramway Museum

17

Omnibus Co Ltd), and then been taken over by BET in 1905. Working along Hagley Road and to Harborne, these omnibus services ran until 5 October 1907, after which neither the locals, who complained about the noise, nor the City Surveyor, who complained about the damage they did to the macadam roads, missed them. The same could be said for the Tramways Department, which then had a temporary monopoly of powered road public transport in the City.

1903: CONSTRUCTION, PREPARATION AND MANOEUVRING

The Birmingham Corporation Act, 1903, empowered the Corporation itself to operate tramways. Ahead was the massive task of reconstructing and electrifying the tramways in a number of districts, as well as assuming operational responsibility for other routes. The districts concerned were Aston, Balsall Heath, Perry Barr & Saltley, Dudley Road, Pebble Mill Road, King's Norton & Handsworth and Small Heath. Of most pressing concern was the Aston route, which the Corporation was due to be operating from 1 January 1904. Here a new tramway would have to be constructed in Steelhouse Lane, the whole route equipped for overhead electric traction, and tramcars and a depot provided. The electric feeder cables were supplied and installed by Callender & Co, the power being obtained from Aston Manor Borough Council, supplied from its Chester Road generating station at the rate of 1.5d per unit. This arrangement would be in force from the opening of the tramway until 31 December 1906, by which time the Corporation's own power station in Summer Lane would be in operation. A 7,000sq yd site for the erection of a depot was obtained at the corner of Miller Street and Elkington Street. This belonged to the Governors of King Edward's Grammar School, and was obtained for £4,963. The

site would permit construction of a depot that would also serve an intended route to Perry Barr; the work was undertaken by Messrs Smith & Pitt for £7,321. As the year progressed the pace of events accelerated. The significant events, as with the years that followed, are highlighted below in diary style.

9 June — The gap in BET's Birmingham tramways portfolio has been the Aston lines. On this date they obtain a 21-year lease of all the tramways in Aston when they have been electrified by the UDC.

11 August — Royal Assent is given to the Birmingham Corporation Act, 1903. Section 50 of this contains the following: 'The Corporation may provide and run Omnibuses in prolongation of any tramway route in the City, the extension of which may be contemplated by the Corporation, and may demand and take tolls or fares for the use of such Omnibuses.'

1 October — The Corporation makes a significant appointment. Alfred Baker, late Chief Officer of London County Council Tramways, is made General Manager of the newly-formed Birmingham Corporation Tramways Department. He has seen the LCC through from the end of its horse tramways to the construction and inauguration of electrified routes using the conduit system, the first line of which opened on 15 May this year. One consideration in appointing Mr Baker may be the Corporation's enduring interest in the conduit system of current collection. Unbeknownst to the Corporation, he hates it, and quickly disabuses his new employers of its advantages with tales of its high initial cost and operational difficulties. Commensurate with the task awaiting him at Birmingham, Alfred Baker's starting salary is set at £1,300 per annum, rising in annual increments of £100 to £1,500. A Mr C. W. Hill, described as

Right: Birmingham Corporation's modest beginnings as an electric tramway operator were more than matched by company activities. On 29 March 1904 CBT opened a route between Small Heath and Yardley, where expectant crowds have gathered while last minute checks are made.
National Tramway Museum

Left: Twenty bogie tramcars were purchased by Birmingham Corporation from the Electric Railway & Tramway Carriage Works Ltd of Preston, for the commencement of its electric tramway service on 4 January 1904. Based in Miller Street depot, the cars worked from Steelhouse Lane to Aston Brook Street.
UEC Co/IAL

having 'considerable experience of car construction and electrical work', is appointed as Assistant Manager, at a salary of £200 per annum. Temporary offices for the Manager are taken at 254A Corporation Street.

October — Starting the retaliation to BET, the Corporation serves notices on CBT this month, signifying its intention to purchase that part of CBT's undertaking within the City.

29 December — Construction work on the Corporation's first tramway as an operator has been proceeding for most of the year. On this date the Board of Trade inspects the reconstructed Aston route, and certifies it fit for public use.

31 December — All that remains is for the Corporation to take possession of the leased portion of the Aston route, and this day the lease of the tramways between Old Square and the Aston boundary expires. A new era of tramway operation in the City can begin tomorrow.

1904: Opening

1 January — Birmingham Corporation is due to commence operation of the Aston route, but concern is expressed that on the following day, Saturday 2 January, a large football crowd is expected in the City, and there might be risks in operating a new and untried tramway under such circumstances. As a compromise, Aston Manor Borough Council suggests that its steam tramcars continue to run into Old Square until 3 January 1904, which is agreed.

4 January — The Tramways Department commences a service of tramcars between Steelhouse Lane and Aston Brook Street using 20 tramcars and one new depot, Miller Street, with a capacity of 24 cars. The tramcars, Nos 1-20, were built by the Electric Railway & Tramway Carriage Works Ltd of Preston, with electrical equipment by Dick, Kerr & Co Ltd, and are open-topped bogie double-deckers, seating 56 (28 upper, 28 lower) and costing £537 10s each. In describing the livery adopted, the Tramways Committee notes: 'They are painted in blue and white colours, which will distinguish them from others in the City.' Advertising will be permitted on the cars, this being handled by an agent, J. W Courtenay of London, who will pay £24 10s per car for the right to do so for seven years.

29 March — CBT opens a new electric tramway between Victoria Park, Small Heath, and Yardley. This has required detailed agreement with the Corporation, as it involves both new tramway construction and the reconstruction and electrification of lines within the City. The new portion of line was built at a cost of £7,610, and that part from Station Street to Victoria Park, Small Heath was renewed and electrified jointly by CBT and the Corporation. Under an agreement signed on 1 June, track relaying is undertaken by the Corporation, with the CBT paying 15% annual interest on the cost of the work until its lease expires on 31 December 1906. Installation of the overhead electric system is the responsibility of CBT, the Corporation having the right to purchase this on expiry of lease at 'the value at the time of purchase'. Agreement is also reached over joint and through working of the route by the CBT and the Corporation from 1 January 1907 until 30 June 1911.

15 June — The last steam tramcars run between the Handsworth/West Bromwich boundary at the Woodman Inn and the cable tramway terminus at the New Inns, this will allow for electrification of the route by Handsworth UDC.

16 June — Birmingham Corporation extends its Aston Brook route to Aston Cross by running over Aston Manor UDC tracks.

22 June — King's Norton & Northfield UDC had obtained powers to build a tramway in an Act of 1901. This had opened in part on 20 May when CBT began an overhead electric tramway service between Navigation Street and Breedon Cross, worked from Dawlish Road depot. The whole tramway is now completed, and is duly inspected by Col Yorke and Mr Trotter of the Board of Trade, being pronounced fit for public use.

23 June — Following its successful inspection the day before, the King's Norton & Northfield UDC's tramway is formally opened. The line runs along the Pershore Road from the City boundary, through Stirchley to Cotteridge, and is worked by CBT in conjunction with the Bristol Road route, which it joins at Pebble Mill Road. The permanent way is the work of R. W. Blackwell & Co Ltd, the feeder cables by Callender & Co, and the whole work cost nearly £40,000. A lease on the line is granted until 30 June 1911. Cotteridge depot, 75ft by 50ft 6in, capacity 12 tramcars, has been built by W. Harvey Gibbs of King's Heath, and opens the same day.

July — CBT introduces a new scheme to encourage employees to deal with electric wire breakage. The Manager, Mr Conaty, offers prizes every three months to the best examples brought to his attention. The winner so far is an employee who mended a breakage in just 16 seconds!

September — Already looking to improve its standard of service, the Corporation fits tramcar No 16 with an experimental top cover.

9 September — South Staffordshire Tramways (Lessee) Co

(BET) begins a service with electric tramcars from Station Road, Handsworth to West Bromwich and the Black Country, replacing steam traction, but this is stopped by Handsworth UDC, which cuts the overhead, and blocks the track with a steam roller, because the company has not signed a lease on the line! This is resolved by 30 September when BET, through the Birmingham & Midland Tramways Co Ltd, signs an agreement with Handsworth concerning the running of electric tramcars through to New Inns. The service begins on 1 October. Two more routes are opened by the Birmingham & Midland company before the year's end:

- 24 November — Edmund Street-Smethwick-Oldbury-Dudley, replacing steam trams;
- 31 December — new branch of the Edmund Street-Dudley route, to Heath Street, Soho.

19 September — CBT replaces steam trams from Aston Cross to Witton by electric cars and, by arrangement with Corporation, works through to Steelhouse Lane. The company opens two more electric lines and a route extension in the following months:

- 27 October — Six Ways-Victoria Road-Park Road;
- 14 November — Salford Bridge-Aston Cross-Gravelly Hill (using single-deck cars owing to a low railway bridge at Aston station);
- 22 December — Six Ways-Park Road route extended to Lichfield Road.

26 November — Aside from all of the above tramway developments, the Birmingham & Midland Motor Omnibus Co Ltd (BMMO) is formed and registered this day by the Birmingham Motor Express Co Ltd (itself formed 1903), in an attempt to raise capital by floating shares. Apart from the Corporation's transport activities, this company will come to have a great impact upon public transport in the City.

1905: PLANNING FOR EXPANSION

17 January — Birmingham Corporation signs a wide-ranging agreement with CBT which includes provisions for the reconstruction of the tramways leased to the company. It is agreed that these be reconstructed in the following order:

- Saltley & Nechells
- King's Heath
- Moseley Road
- Stratford Road.

Specifications for this work are prepared by the City Surveyor and Tramways Manager, and the following tenders accepted:

- Permanent way reconstruction: Dick, Kerr & Co Ltd, Preston, £42,261 15s 1d;
- Tram rails: Bolckow, Vaughan & Co, Middlesbrough, £5 10s per ton;
- Special trackwork: Hadfield's Steel Foundry Co, Sheffield, £1,708 10s.

RECONSTRUCTION OF ASTON BRIDGE SUNDAY MARCH 25
A Great Engineering Feat.
This Bridge, weighing 300 tons, was placed in position in 15 minutes.

The work is to be completed by the end of October 1905. The agreement, endorsed by the Council on 7 February, also includes the purchase by the Corporation of Kyotts Lake Road depot and Works; this comes into effect on 1 July 1906.

23 February — Reconstruction of the steam tramway track from Station Street to Small Heath allows CBT to open a through service to Yardley.

March — After a successful experiment since last September, Corporation tramcars Nos 1-10 are fitted with top covers, one using that from car No 16, which reverts to open-topped condition. Nos 11-20 receive top covers in July 1907.

31 March —The first full-year figures for the Corporation Tramways show the following:

- Length of route (Steelhouse Lane-Aston Cross):

City lines	1 mile 66yd
Aston lines	581yd

- Corporation receipts:

Corporation receipts:	£17,133 19s 0d
CBT Co Ltd receipts:	£2,744 14s 2d
(less Corporation receipts on Aston lines:	£3,789 9s 11d)
= combined net receipts:	£16,089 3s 3d
• Passengers carried	4,709,798
• Miles run in Birmingham	216,235
• Miles run in Aston	50,291

The gross profit on the Steelhouse Lane route to date is £8,764 1s 2d.

April — Heartened by these profits, and with new routes planned for when the majority of the company leases on tramways in the City expire on 31 December 1906,

Birmingham Corporation orders 200 four-wheel open-top tramcars from Dick, Kerr & Co Ltd, at a total cost of £110,411 12s, including spare parts. That for 150 of the cars is subsequently changed early in 1906.

24 May — Birmingham & Midland Tramways Co (BET) extends its Edmund Street-Dudley branch route from Heath Street, Soho, to Soho station.

1 June — BMMO formally takes over 15 double-deck motor omnibuses formerly operated by its parent company, the Birmingham Midland Express Co, on the Hagley Road and Harborne routes; also some 100 horse omnibuses and 1,000 horses previously worked by CBT and the Birmingham & Midland Tramways Ltd. Four days later, on 5 June, the Birmingham Midland Express Co directors resign and are replaced by BET nominees, giving the latter effective control of BMMO.

August — The Birmingham Corporation Act, 1905, gains Royal Assent. It authorises work on nine tramways on the following routes: Lodge Road, Bordesley Green, Holloway Head, Bolton Road, Thimble Mill Lane, Leopold Street, Saltley Road & Washwood Heath, Alum Rock and Cannon

Hill Park. Together these total 21 miles 2 furlongs 44.43 chains of tramway, and work on them is subsequently allocated to three contractors:

- William Griffiths & Co (Lodge Road)   £14,289 17s 8d
- Dick, Kerr & Co Ltd (Cannon Hill Park)   £6,235 9s 9d
- John Aird & Co (the remainder)   £43,698 15s 10d

These sums exclude the cost of rails and paving materials. On this subject, the Council has received requests for residents in Balsall Heath and Islington Row to have their tramway routes paved with wooden blocks rather than granite setts. Upon investigation, it is found that the annual maintenance cost of wood blocks exceeds that of setts by some £200-£250 per mile of single line, and an attempt to require a section of Monument Lane to be paved with wood blocks is defeated at the Council Meeting held on 10 April 1906.

13 August — King's Norton & Northfield UDC signs an agreement with CBT to take over the Pershore Road tramway.

29 September — A suite of offices is taken for the Tramways Department in the former Wesleyan & General Assurance Society building in Corporation Street, for five years at £350 per annum.

24 October — A memorial is presented to the Tramways Committee by Councillor Tonks from ratepayers along the route of the cable tramway, complaining about the noise it makes.

Winter — On advice from Alfred Baker, the Tramways Committee adopts the span wire system of overhead construction with side poles for all its converted and new tramways, with the exception of parts of the Balsall Heath and Nechells routes (where bracket arm construction is advisable), and Corporation Street, between Martineau Street and Old Square (where the span wires will be attached to rosettes on the buildings). The contract for installing this overhead equipment, on the equivalent of about 44 miles of single track, amounts to £27,231, and is awarded to Dick, Kerr & Co Ltd.

1906: New Routes and the End of an Era

Winter — The City Surveyor reports on the excessive damage being done to macadam roads by motor omnibuses, the rear double-ringed tyres of which suck out fine material, especially in wet weather. A number of roads, including Hagley Road, are resurfaced.

January — Following representations, the Board of Trade rules in favour of the use of top-covered tramcars on inland routes without steep gradients or exposure to high winds. As a result, the order for 200 four-wheel open-top tramcars from Dick, Kerr & Co Ltd placed in April 1905 is changed, with 150 of the cars to be modified. They are to be delivered with top covers, and have four-window saloons, like the bogie cars 1-20. In addition, they are to have radial rather than rigid wheel trucks, and be fitted with magnetic track brakes. These modifications add an extra £23,500 to the cost of the tramcars.

25 March — BET's Aston Cross-Gravelly Hill service has been worked by single-deck tramcars until this date. Double-decker cars are now used owing to the rebuilding of a low railway bridge at Aston station.

March-June — The first 50 of the 200 tramcars ordered in April 1905 from Dick, Kerr & Co Ltd are delivered. They arrive in two batches: Nos 21-40 and Nos 41-70, all being in service by June. They are standard British four-wheeler,

Below: Tramway services to Nechells would always provide superlatives. The first was as Birmingham's last horse tramway, which closed on 30 September 1906. This was immediately replaced by horse omnibuses, until track reconstruction around Albert Street in the City allowed Corporation electric trams to run from 24 November 1906.
Commercial Postcard/Author's Collection

Above: For the first few years of electric tramway operation in Birmingham the Corporation shared some routes and lines with CBT. Here at Aston Cross in May 1906 a company car works City-bound down Park Road whilst a CBT 'Radial' class car waits in Lichfield Road. *Commercial Postcard/ Author's Collection*

Centre right: Completion of a loop of track in Albert Street allowed Birmingham Corporation to commence an electric tramway service to Bordesley Green via Fazeley Street. Car No 52 of 1905 is seen at Bordesley Green c1912 when the car had been fitted with a top cover. To the right is Mr Burn, the tobacconist. *Commercial Postcard/ Author's Collection*

Right: The Bristol Road route boasted long straight sections, and, in its early years, was almost devoid of other traffic. CBT car No 207 of 1904 is seen just north of Priory Road on this poor quality postcard franked 22 September 1906. In 1912 the car became Corporation tramcar No 467 and remained in service until 1939. *Commercial Postcard/ Author's Collection*

three-window, open-topped double-deckers, seating 48 (6/22).

10 April — The Tramways Committee reports that the reconstruction of the tramways on the Saltley & Nechells, King's Heath, Moseley Road and Stratford Road routes has been successfully carried out by Dick, Kerr & Co Ltd. The Committee also notes the need to 'provide depots in convenient parts of the City where the cars could be properly housed and cleaned', and has accordingly acquired sites for this purpose in Rosebery Street, Moseley Road, Coventry Road, and Washwood Heath Road. Depots for the first two sites have been designed by Mr F. B. Osborn, and for the latter two by Ingall, Son & Mitton. A total of £21,970 has been spent on acquiring the sites, and building contracts to the value of £72,231 have been placed for their construction. In addition, Hadfields Ltd has supplied £3,999 2s 6d worth of special trackwork for the depots, and lighting has been supplied by Mr E. M. Redfern for £463 7s.

14 April — Birmingham Corporation opens an electric tramway to Lodge Road (Foundry Road) from Edmund Street (Route 32 from 1915). A new depot in Rosebery Street, Brookfields, is also opened, with a capacity of 75 tramcars (later expanded to 85). The site occupies 4,500sq yd, and is purchased for £5,194; the contractor is W. Hopkins, and the contract price is £18,438. An area of 607sq yd is set aside on the site for the building of an electricity sub-station.

7 May — CBT opens an extension of its Aston service from Six Ways to Finch Road on Lozells Road. On 3 June this is further extended to Villa Cross.

30 June — The leases on Birmingham & Midland Tramways Co's routes expire; joint operation with the Corporation follows.

1 July — Birmingham Corporation opens an electric tramway between Heath Street, Soho, and Bearwood (Route 29 from 1915), and purchases and takes possession of Kyotts Lake Road depot and Works from CBT.

August — The first of the revised order for 150 four-wheel tramcars enters service. They are numbered 71-220 and seat 52 (28/24).

30 September — The last horse tram service in the City, Albert Street-Nechells, is withdrawn.

10 October — Birmingham Corporation's power station in Summer Lane is officially opened. This has been erected on the site of the former General Hospital, and provides four kinds of supply:

- 220V and 440V dc to private customers;
- 440V dc to a trunk mains system;
- 5,000V three-phase ac to City sub-stations;
- 550V dc to overhead electric tramways.

17 October — The Corporation opens an electric tramway between Navigation Street and Dudley Road, Ladywood (Route 33 from 1915).

November — The Tramways Committee orders 50 more open-top, four-wheel tramcars from Dick, Kerr & Co Ltd.

26 November — Birmingham Corporation opens an electric tramway between Albert Street, Fazeley Street and Blake Lane (Bordesley Green) (Route 11 from 1915). It also opens Coventry Road tramcar depot (capacity 94 tramcars, later increased to 106). This stands on a 5,908sq yd site bought for £7,534, and has been built by W. Cunliffe for £20,746.

22 December — The Corporation pays CBT for the tracks in Balsall Heath, which were laid down before the area was incorporated into the City in 1891.

31 December — Last day of running for steam tramcars in the City, after 24 years. All CBT leases expire on this date, save for the routes on the Bristol and Pershore Roads, and that to Handsworth.

1907: A GREATER TRAMWAY AND A DISASTER

1 January — The Corporation opens nine tramway routes (their later route numbers are shown in brackets):

- Station Street-Oldknow Road-Bordesley Park Road-Bolton Road (22)
- Navigation Street (Queen's Head Hotel)-Cannon Hill Park (37)
- Hill Street-Leopold Street-Balsall Heath-King's Heath (Vicarage Road) — extended to Alcester Lanes End on 12 January (40)
- Martineau Street-Nechells (7)
- Station Street-Hay Mills Bridge-Yardley (16)
- Station Street-Stratford Road (College Road) (18)
- Station Street-Stoney Lane (Esme Road) (4)
- Martineau Street-Alum Rock Road (Highfield Road) (8)
- Martineau Street-Phillips Street (City boundary) (6)

The day is full of incidents, with many dewirings caused by inexperienced drivers, who drive too cautiously for many. There is also an accident. At just past 8.00pm one James Smith, boarding a Sparkhill tram in Station Street, overbalances and falls into the road, suffering a nasty scalp wound. The Corporation also acquires CBT's running depot and administration centre at Kyotts Lake Road, off the Stratford Road, and opens Moseley Road tram depot, with a capacity of 75 tramcars (later increased to 77). This is built on a 6,202sq yd site bought for £6,902, the contractor being T. Lowe & Sons, at a cost of £22,220. A portion of the site is left for later extensions. On the same day CBT begins a service from Phillips Street to Six Ways (Aston) and Witton, but this ceases on 4 January, being replaced by one from Phillips Street to Chain Walk (the Handsworth UDC boundary).

March — The last of the Corporation's revised order of 150 four-wheel tramcars enters service. They are used on the Coventry Road, Moseley Road and Washwood Heath routes.

March-May — The 50 tramcars ordered by the Corporation in November 1906 enter service. They are numbered 221-270.

22 April — CBT's route to Salford Bridge is extended to Erdington and worked jointly by the company and the Corporation. (This becomes Route 2 from 1915.)

2 May — The tramway to Washwood Heath, as far as Sladefield Road (Route 9 from 1915) opens, as does that from Chain Walk to Perry Barr; the latter is worked by the

TRAM TERM'S. STONEY LANE.

Above: Among the new tramway services introduced by Birmingham Corporation on 1 January 1907 was that from Station Street to Stoney Lane, Sparkbrook. Here No 160 of 1906, one of the first batch of Corporation tramcars to be fitted with a top cover from new, waits at the Stoney Lane terminus by Doris Road. *Commercial Postcard/Author's Collection*

Below: There is an air of finality in this shot of CBT locomotive No 87 and its trailer working one of the last steam tram services between Old Square and Saltley late in 1906. *IAL*

In Remembrance of

THE BIRMINGHAM & DISTRICT OLD STEAM TRAMS

WHICH STARTED
SERVICE
NOVEMBER 25th,
1884.

PASSING AWAY
OWING
TO AN ELECTRIC
SHOCK
JANUARY 1st, 1907.

" Let not ambition mock their useful toils,
Their homely joys and destiny obscure."

Photo by]

[P. King.

Above: Postcards of this kind were issued in many parts of the country when horse and steam tramways 'succumbed' or 'passed away owing' to an electric shock. This one commemorated the passing of steam trams in Birmingham and shows a CBT car on the Saltley-Old Square route.
Commercial Postcard/Author's Collection

Below: Corporation electric tramway operation expanded rapidly after the expiry of the CBT leases on 31 December 1906. Many new routes were introduced the following day, but that to Erdington was delayed until 22 April 1907 owing to a failure to agree terms for through running. Car No 57 was the first to run that day and is seen outside the newly-built 'Terminus Restaurant'. *Tramway & Light Railway World/IAL*

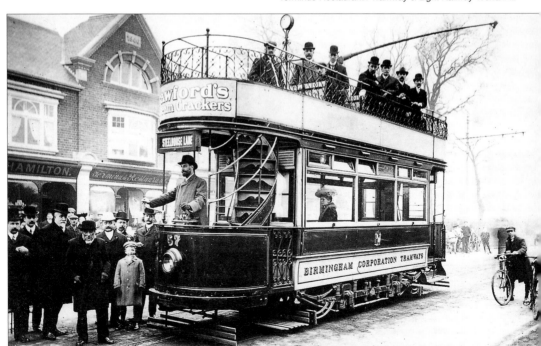

Above: The Corporation's Station Street-Yardley tramcar service was introduced on 1 January 1907. Car No 34 is seen in Coventry Road during the first few months, running a short-working to Small Heath Park. *Commercial Postcard/Author's Collection*

Below: At the rear of Small Heath Park runs Byron Road, an extension of Bolton Road, where car No 46 was photographed in 1907. This was the closest tramway service to the massive BSA works, which was just the other side of the GWR main line, in Armoury Road. *Commercial Postcard/Author's Collection*

Corporation on behalf of Handsworth UDC. The Tramways Department also acquires Birchfield Road depot (capacity 20 tramcars), and opens Washwood Heath depot (capacity 48 tramcars, later increased to 66). Washwood Heath depot is built for £10,827 by the builder T. Johnson on a 9,936sq yd site bought for £2,340. A portion of the site is left for later extensions.

23 May — Birmingham Corporation begins a tramway service from Martineau Street through Aston to Chain Walk, the Handsworth boundary (route 6 from 1915).

7 August — An experimental tramway service from Martineau Street to Saltley, via Great Lister Street, commences, but is not successful and ends on 11 September.

1 October — Birmingham's first major tramway accident: tramcar No 22, driven by Inspector Thomas Hall, descends the 1 in 17 gradient in Warstone Lane at speed, and overturns on the curve into Hingeston Street at the foot of the hill. Unfortunately, two passengers, William Henry James and William Percy James, of Holte Street, Witton, are killed, and

17 others injured. The resultant Board of Trade Inquiry, held on 10 October, determines the cause as a failure of the magnetic brake, due to a faulty rheostat. As a long-term consequence of this accident, 54 cars in the same class are fitted with Maley track brakes by 1910.

November — Another 30 open-top, four-wheel tramcars are ordered from Dick, Kerr & Co Ltd. Following the Warstone Lane accident on 1 October, Alfred Baker has visited Leeds on two occasions to witness tests of the Maley track brake. This is a combination mechanical track brake and electro-magnetic brake, both acting on the rails. It can be operated mechanically or electrically, either from regenerative power from the motors, or, in the case of motor failure, directly from the overhead supply. The Board of Trade would only permit three of the new cars to be so fitted, but the General Manager hopes to obtain the Board's permission for all 30 to have them.

26 November — Tramways in Moor Street and Digbeth are inspected by the Board of Trade and certified safe for public use.

Left: Coventry Road depot opened on 26 November 1906. It stood on a 5,908sq yd site, bought for £7,534, and was built by W. Cunliffe for £20,746. Its capacity was 94 tramcars (later increased to 106), and in 1908 included the then new car No 279. *Commercial Postcard/Author's Collection*

Above: Birmingham's saddest tramway event for many a year came on 1 October 1907 when car No 22 ran out of control down the 1 in 17 gradient in Warstone Road and overturned on the curve into Hingeston Street. Passengers William Henry James and William Percy James were killed and 17 others injured. The cause was traced to a failure of the magnetic brake due to a faulty rheostat. *Commercial Postcard/Author's Collection*

5 December — The tracks in Moor Street and Digbeth are opened, allowing through services across the City on an experimental basis. The routes tried are:

- Erdington-Alcester Lanes End
- Nechells-Small Heath Park
- Saltley-Sparkbrook.

1908: HOUSING PROBLEMS

March-April — The 30 tramcars ordered in November 1907 enter service; they are numbered 271-300.

Spring — On the recommendation of the General Manager, the Tramways Committee adopts a Merit Stripe Scheme. Under this scheme, after three years' continuous service, Inspectors, Motormen and Conductors earn a stripe which carries an extra 2d in pay per day. Awarded at the Manager's discretion, the stripe can also be withdrawn for bad conduct.

1 April — King's Heath depot in Silver Street, a former steam tramcar depot (capacity 20 tramcars), is taken over by the Corporation. At around this time the capacity of Miller Street depot is also increased (from 24 to 54 tramcars). Extra land was purchased in December 1907, and the site has been developed as the main permanent way centre, with workshops and a foundry. Additional shedding for 30 tramcars has been erected by A. J. Teal & Co Ltd, for £5,620.

8 April — Tramlines from High Street/Bradford Street to Bordesley and Camp Hill come into use. They are connected with the Stratford Road service. A service to Hall Green is also introduced (Route 17 from 1915).

Autumn — The condition of the Bristol Road tramway beyond Speedwell Road has become ever more unsatisfactory, arising from the nature of the subsoil, and the lack of drainage on the road. Accordingly, the Corporation decides to reconstruct this section of road and tramway entirely, incorporating drainage, at a cost of £23,000. Until the expiry of CBT's lease on the tramway on 30 June 1911, the company will pay £2,300 per annum towards this work.

Left: For 36 years Birmingham Corporation celebrated Royal and national events by running special illuminated trams around the City. The first of these was prepared for the visit of King Edward VII and Queen Alexandra to open the new University buildings at Edgbaston on 7 July 1909. Based around No 266, the blazing message 'WELCOME TO OUR KING & QUEEN' was shot by a Mr Twigg as it passed through Nechells ahead of a service car. *Commercial Postcard/ Author's Collection*

1909: CONSOLIDATION AND GUN LAW

1 January — New depot accommodation allows Birchfield Road depot to be closed.

9 May — By-law No 20, passed by the Council on 2 March, is modified following representations made by the local gun trade. It now reads: 'No person shall travel in or on any car with loaded firearms.'

July — Birmingham Council approves the purchase of the cable tramway in Handsworth, after prolonged and expensive negotiations. CBT is granted a short lease on the line, until 30 June 1911.

6 September — The Corporation begins a new tramway service from High Street via Rea Street to Moseley Road.

8 December — A through tramway service from Martineau Street to Perry Barr (Route 6 from 1915) is started by the Corporation by arrangement with CBT.

1910: ECONOMIES AND PREPARATION FOR FURTHER EXPANSION

Some tramcars in the fleet have been fitted with traction meters, which enable the drivers to check their current consumption. In the year to 31 March 1911 this will show a saving of £5,423 on power expenses.

December — An order is placed with Dick, Kerr & Co Ltd for 60 four-wheel, top-covered, double-deck tramcars, with bodies by the United Electric Car Co Ltd, Preston. These are to be fitted with vestibules, and to have trilateral dash panels, all standard features on subsequent Birmingham tramcars. The cars are needed for the Handsworth, King's Norton and Selly Oak routes, all to be taken over in July 1911.

Left: Birmingham's shortest-lived electric tramway route was that from Dale End to Nechells, which ran for seven years less than the horse tramway it replaced. Mostly single-track, this 1910 view shows a lone tramcar working along Nechells Park Road while a boy poses for the camera with his hoop. *Commercial Postcard/Author's Collection*

3. 1911-1920: Complete Control and Services for All

Above: Corporation tramway services to King's Heath began on 1 January 1907 and were extended 11 days later to a new terminus at Alcester Lanes End. There, c1912, car No 73 loads for its return to the City.
Commercial Postcard/Author's Collection

The events of the 1910s would test the resolve of everyone involved in the newly established Birmingham Corporation Transport. Solely a tramway undertaking at the start of this period, the Corporation acquired firstly complete control of tramway services in the City, then a monopoly, as the BET-controlled CBT was finally laid to rest. The goalposts moved too, for in the midst of these changes the 'pitch' grew larger, as the Greater Birmingham Scheme and enlarged Council took effect. There were new districts to be served, and the scale of the Tramways Department's task was immense. New routes were opened — Handsworth, Selly Oak, Cotteridge (ex-CBT), Yardley, Bordesley Green, Hagley Road, Acocks Green — and others extended — Witton, Lozells, Washwood Heath. An additional 275 new tramcars were acquired to operate these services, plus 61 of the best ex-CBT ones; a new depot was built at Hockley, and Cotteridge depot greatly enlarged.

From 1913 bogie tramcars were once again favoured, and a start was made on fitting top covers to the entire fleet. Limited experiments were also conducted with first class tramcars. The Tramways Department also became a motor omnibus operator, firstly as an extension to the Bristol Road tramway, and then through the acquisition of six BMMO services to the west of the City, plus 30 vehicles and garage

from which to work them. Four additional services were introduced, but the deleterious effect of solid-tyred wheels on the City's roads brought rebukes from the Public Works Department.

Just as things were settling down a little, the nation declared war. This bit deepest in 1916 and 1917, as both material and human resources were depleted and scarce. Members of staff were pressed into military service, and women workers taken on in large numbers. Fuel shortages caused the cancellation or suspension of omnibus services, and route numbers were introduced to help passengers cope with reduced street lighting. In the midst of the war, there were calls for all-night tramway services, and trials were conducted with single-deck tramcars hauling trailer cars. Eventually, fares had to rise, twice, in an attempt to stem a decline in revenue. Despite these difficulties, prudent

The New Inns, Handsworth.

Above: The South Staffordshire Tramways Co ran electric tramcars through to the New Inns, Handsworth, from 1 October 1904, but until 1 July 1911 completion of a journey into the city by tram had to be by means of CBT's cable cars. These can be seen in the distance behind South Staffs Brush bogie car No 14. *Commercial Postcard/ Author's Collection*

Left: Together with the expired leases held by CBT, on 1 July 1911 Birmingham Corporation also came into possession of a number of the company's tramcars, including No 156 of 1901, which became BCT No 504. Old-fashioned and hard-riding it remained in service with the Corporation only until January 1924. *Commercial Postcard/ Author's Collection*

CABLE CAR'S FAREWELL.

Farewell, kind friends, I'm going
To the scrap heap, so they say;
The worthy City Fathers
Think too long I've held the sway.
They deem me old and ugly,
In fact, not up to date;
If ever love they had for me
Their love's turned into hate.

This city's known as "Forward"—
A motto that means well;
'Tis that what makes them anxious
The cable car to sell.
Some say that I'm not handsome,
But most of them agree
When electric cars they take my place
Improvement there will be.

And now before I leave you
Kind friends take my advice;
And you, both guards and drivers
Who all have acted nice—
Give out a hearty welcome
When the new friend does appear;
For though his name's Electric Car
To your welfare he's sincere

Composed by John Bryan.

Above: John Bryan's lament for the passing of the Handsworth cable trams was a hot seller in the summer of 1911. The last cable tramcar ran on 30 June that year, and the one shown was advertising the LNWR's 'Greatly Improved & Accelerated Service' introduced just 12 months earlier. *Commercial Postcard/Author's Collection*

Right: The Greater Birmingham Scheme came into effect on 9 November 1911, bringing Moseley Village, seen here, within the City boundary. Before this date the Corporation had worked the tramway down Alcester Road to King's Heath on behalf of King's Norton & Northfield UDC. No 91 is about to pass under an overhead feeder and section break. *Commercial Postcard/ Author's Collection*

management brought the Tramways Department through the war, and a notable milestone was reached when the 1917/8 end-of-year figures showed that the annual revenue had topped £1 million.

With the Armistice came the chance to develop services further. No new tramcars had been ordered since 1913, something quickly rectified. The City Council also began an ambitious programme to improve the City approach roads. Its Arterial Roads Scheme constructed these as dual carriageways, and left space for tramways along the central reservations. Tramways constructed along both Pebble Mill Road and the Tyburn Road were the first built to this pattern. More would follow, and the future for tramway and omnibus operation in Birmingham looked bright.

1911: COMPLETING CONTROL

April-June — The 60 tramcars ordered from Dick, Kerr & Co Ltd in December 1910 are delivered. They are numbered 301-360 and seat 52 (upper saloon 28, lower saloon 24).

23 May — The Tramways Committee's report to the Council notes that it has given instructions for every tramcar to be fitted with a top cover before the winter. The single-line tramway in Garrison Lane and Watery Lane, Bordesley, is to be doubled, at an estimated cost of £1,100.

June — After discussion with representatives of the London & North Western and Midland railways, a siding and shelter has been provided for passengers on the Bolton Road, Coventry Road and Yardley routes, who previously had to wait in the middle of the road.

MOSELEY VILLAGE

June — Appraisal of the 30 tramcars used on the King's Norton and Selly Oak routes, to be acquired from CBT next month, shows them to be in a poor and generally unsatisfactory condition. As a result, the December 1910 order placed with Dick, Kerr & Co Ltd is extended by a further 40 cars, of slightly modified design.

30 June — CBT's lease on the Handsworth cable tramway expires.

1 July — Birmingham Corporation has complete control of tramway services in its area. It assumes operation of the former CBT routes, and three new electric routes begin:

- Handsworth (ex-cable traction) (Route 23 from 1915)
- Selly Oak (Route 35 from 1915)
- Cotteridge (Route 36 from 1915).

The Handsworth route has cost £1,181 to electrify, but uses cable tramway tracks initially, as there has not been time to reconstruct it. This does not happen until the latter part of 1912, when £40,515 is spent upon the work. The Tramways Department also acquires the title and use of Albion depot in Holyhead Road, which holds just eight tramcars, Bournbrook depot in Dawlish Road, which holds 42 tramcars, renting it from CBT for six months at £2 per day, and Cotteridge depot, capacity eight tramcars. Hockley depot, capacity 104 tramcars, is also acquired on this date, but is immediately closed for conversion to electric traction. On the same day the advertising contract with Mr J. W. Courtenay of London is renewed for a further seven years, at £20 per car per annum.

25 July — Birmingham City Council approves the Corporation's purchase of the whole CBT undertaking, but stops short of approving the purchase of any tramways outside the existing City limits as it lacks the powers to do so, and does not wish to bind the new Council to this. Accordingly, CBT remains in control for a short while.

November — The first of the additional 40 tramcars ordered from Dick, Kerr & Co Ltd in June enters service. They are numbered 361-400 and are identical to the other cars in the batch, except for having 3in longer platforms to accommodate a different staircase design, and a handbrake spindle which requires the fitting of a projecting dished metal cowl to the vestibule, something else that would become a standard Birmingham tramcar characteristic feature. The last of the cars enters service in February 1912.

28 November — One of the enlarged Council's first duties is to approve the Corporation's purchase of CBT.

31 December — CBT's operation of tramways in Birmingham ends.

1912: MONOPOLY

1 January — Birmingham Corporation purchases and takes over all of the former CBT tramways in its newly enlarged area, at a net cost of £145,476. It also acquires 61 of the company's 100 tramcars, and six depots, at Dawlish Road, Cotteridge, Perry Barr, Hockley and Yardley, the latter being closed this date, and sold in 1916. College Road permanent way yard in Sparkhill is also acquired, and is used for tramcar

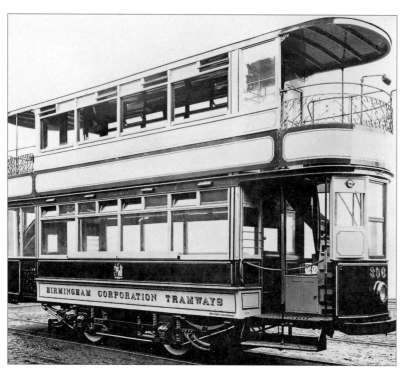

Left: The major expansion of Birmingham Corporation Tramways which took place on 1 July 1911 required many additional tramcars. Sixty cars were ordered in December 1910, and this was extended by a further 40 cars in June 1911. The batch being known as the '301' class, No 396 seen here entered service early in 1912. *UEC Co/ National Tramway Museum*

Above: The original terminus for Short Heath tramcars was at Stockland Green, by the junction of Slade and Stockland roads. In 1912, car No 223 was surrounded there by a rural idyll on the City's suburban edge, but this would not last for much longer, the land behind had already been let for development. *Commercial Postcard/Author's Collection*

Below: The ornate and decorous bridge above Corporation tramcar No 89 linked the City Art Gallery (right) with its extension (left), which was opened on 19 July 1912. Edmund Street, beneath, was one of the City's busiest tramway termini, for routes to the west and into the Black Country. *Commercial Postcard/Author's Collection*

MOTOR TERMINUS SELLY O

storage, before being disposed of in 1924. New tramway services also begin on the following routes:

- Martineau Street-Six Ways-Witton (Route 3 from 1915)
- Martineau Street-Aston Cross-Witton (Route 3X from 1915)
- Villa Cross-Lichfield Road (Route 5 from 1915).

January — Increased tramway use, and forthcoming routes, such as that to Stockland Green, necessitate a further order for 50 tramcars. This is placed with Dick, Kerr & Co Ltd, for four-wheel, double-deck cars like those of the 361-400 batch of 1911. Again, the bodies will be built by the United Car Co Ltd of Preston.

16 January — The Corporation's purchase of CBT is completed. The Town Clerk reports that the purchase price has been £151,500, plus £681 for stores in hand at Yardley and Bournbrook depots.

31 March — King's Heath depot in Silver Street, the former steam tramcar depot with a capacity of 20 tramcars, acquired on 1 April 1908, is closed.

25 May — BET-controlled BMMO puts three double-deck motor omnibuses into service on the Hagley Road and Harborne routes. They are based on Tilling-Stevens petrol-electric chassis, and operate from a garage in Tennant Street, behind Broad Street.

June — The BET-controlled Birmingham & Midland Tramways Co changes its name to the Birmingham District Power & Traction Co Ltd. It has only a residual interest in tramways, through ownership of eight miles of lines operated by the Corporation.

12 June — Tramlines are extended from Stockland Green to Marsh Lane, Witton. Albion depot is closed, replaced by new accommodation at Hockley depot, which opens the same day.

August — The first of the 50 tramcars ordered in January enters service. They are numbered 401-450 and seat 54 (30/24). The last cars in the batch enter service in March 1913.

7 October — Albion depot is leased to South Staffordshire (Lessee) Tramways Co, until 31 March 1924.

9 October — The South Staffordshire (Lessee) Tramways Co begins a service of through tramcars from Colmore Row to Darlaston via West Bromwich and Wednesbury.

20 November — A new tramway service begins, from Colmore Row to Lozells, via Wheeler Street (Route 24 from 1915) or Hamstead Road (Route 25 from 1915).

Left: On 19 July 1913 Birmingham Corporation exercised the limited powers at its disposal to operate motor omnibus services, to extend the Bristol Road tramway route from Selly Oak to Longbridge and Rednal. On a day early in this service, passengers alighting from Corporation tramcar No 343 could opt to travel on by Corporation motor omnibus No 7. *Commercial Postcard/ Author's Collection*

Right: On 29 November 1913 Birmingham Corporation inaugurated its second 'tramway extension' motor omnibus service, between Selly Oak and Rubery. Possibly on that very day, No 7, laden with schoolboys, poses with its crew and a local man sporting a very generously brimmed hat. *National Motor Museum*

20 December — A new tramway service from Colmore Row to Oxhill Road (Rookery Road) begins (Route 26 from 1915).

1913: THE FIRST OMNIBUS SERVICE

January — A new tramway service between High Street and Yardley begins (Route 15 from 1915).

8 January — An extension to the Gravelly Hill-Lozells route (Route 5 from 1915) is opened from Villa Cross, up Villa Road as far as the Soho Road/Soho Hill junction.

10 January — Track in Livery Street is opened for use as an inward route and loading point for Black Country and Handsworth services. It has cost £3,961 to construct.

March — The Corporation orders 40 bogie tramcars from Dick, Kerr & Co Ltd, with bodies by the United Electric Car Co Ltd. With recent developments in maximum-traction bogies, Alfred Baker believes that these will offer an improved ride, longer service life, and greater seating capacity than four-wheeled cars.

April — BMMO is given a licence for half-hourly services from the Ivy Bush to Quinton, Handsworth and Moseley.

2 April — A new tramway service is introduced linking High Street, Deritend, Bordesley Green (Blake Lane) and

Little Bromwich (Route 12 from 1915). Tracks in Cattell Road, Small Heath, only used for depot workings since 1906, are also brought into passenger use at this time.

20 May — Reporting to the Council, the Tramways Committee finds that, acceding to 'a very considerable demand for improved means of locomotion between Selly Oak, Northfield, and Longbridge', and acknowledging that it is 'actively engaged in preparing a (tramway) scheme for this purpose, which it is hoped will be ready for submission to Parliament next year', it has resolved that 'it is desirable that … a service of Motor Omnibuses should be immediately instituted'. It seeks authorisation to purchase 10 suitable motor omnibuses at a cost not exceeding £10,000. The same report also notes that a memorial and deputation from blind persons, seeking free travel on Corporation tramcars to and from work, has been denied.

June — The Corporation orders 35 more tramcars of the kind ordered in March.

19 July — Introduction of omnibus services: 10 vehicles are placed in service between Selly Oak and Rednal as an extension of the Bristol Road tramway. The omnibuses are open-top Daimler B types, with 40hp petrol engines and fitted with 34-seat bodies (18/16). The vehicles share Dawlish Road

Above: In its penultimate prewar tramway extension, the Corporation opened a new terminus for the Washwood Heath route alongside the Fox & Goose Hotel at Ward End on 20 December 1913. The photographer capturing the scene there has engaged everyone's attention, including those aboard tramcar No 433. *Commercial Postcard/Author's Collection*

Below: A family hurries from Portland Road to board Corporation tramcar No 517, of 1913, City-bound along the Hagley Road in 1914. Oh that the road was so quiet at this point today! The curious fluted gas standard at left was for the burning and venting of sewer gas. *Commercial Postcard/Author's Collection*

depot in Bournbrook. They are pressed into war service in the early weeks of World War 1. The route is unnumbered until March 1916, when it becomes No 5.

5 September — New tramlines and a route along Hagley Road from Navigation Street (Queen's Hotel) to Hagley Road (King's Road) via Five Ways are opened. Lettered H and numbered 34 from 1915, the route has cost £31,503 to construct.

October — The first of the 75 bogie double-deck tramcars ordered in March and June enters service. Numbered 512-586, these top-covered cars seat 62 (upper saloon 34, lower saloon 28). They are the first of a standard pattern of bogie double-deck tramcar that Birmingham will order, the last of the batch entering service in December 1914, the total cost being £40,662. (The fleet numbers between these cars and the last new ones ordered are taken up by 61 tramcars, 451-511, representing a portion of those acquired from CBT which are deemed suitable for refurbishment to Corporation standards.)

4 October — Omnibus Route 7 (General Hospital-Five Ways) introduced. It runs until 31 October and then is combined with Route 1.

25 November — Highgate Road depot opens. It has a capacity of 90 tramcars, and was built at a cost of £21,510.

29 November — An omnibus service commences between Selly Oak and Rubery (numbered 6 from March 1916, and replaced by a tramway extension from 8 February 1926).

20 December — The Washford Heath tramway route is extended from Sladefield Road to the Fox & Goose, at a cost of £7,986.

1914: FIRST CLASS TRAMCARS AND MORE OMNIBUSES

14 February — Agreement is reached between the Corporation and BMMO over operations within the City. BMMO is not to compete with the Corporation within the City, although it may through-run over tramway routes in order to reach outer areas not served by these. Similarly, the Corporation is not to compete with BMMO outside the City. The agreement will come into force as soon as the Corporation obtains an Act authorising it to run a general service of motor omnibuses within the City, and the purchase of certain BMMO assets will follow immediately upon this.

25 February — An experiment with First Class tramcars begins on the Hagley Road route between Navigation Street and Fountain Road. The lower saloons of cars 581-584 have been 'improved'. Double fares are charged to ride in them, ordinary passengers being carried on top. This does not prove a success, and the cars quickly resume ordinary service, before being withdrawn in May.

17 March — Following representations and deputations, the Tramways Committee receives a letter from the All-night Tram Service Joint Associations Movement, asking for the provision of all-night services on the Handsworth, Bearwood, King's Heath, Sparkhill, Yardley and Erdington routes, and

Below: Four tramcars, Nos 581-4, were chosen for an experiment with First Class tram travel on the Hagley Road route between Navigation Street and Fountain Road, beginning on 25 February 1914. The lower saloons were 'improved' with plusher seats and brown curtains, double fares being charged to ride in them. The experiment was not a success, and it was withdrawn in May 1914. No 582 is seen at Fountain Road. *National Tramway Museum*

Above: No sooner had the Corporation inaugurated motor omnibus services than it lost its vehicles, as the chassis from the original 10 Daimlers were pressed into war service. In their place 10 Tilling-Stevens TS3 chassis were acquired, to which the Daimlers' bodies, complete with registration numbers, were fitted. This is No 39, fitted with rudimentary driver protection. *IAL*

for a modified service to be tried on the Alum Rock, Bordesley Green, Nechells and Perry Barr routes. To assess the need for these, the Committee arranges for censuses to be taken at Bordesley Park Road (Coventry Road), Henley Street (Stratford Road), Balsall Heath Road, Moseley Road (King's Heath), the junction of Balsall Heath Road and Longmore Street (Balsall Heath), Dartmouth Street (Erdington), Vyse Street (Handsworth) and Monument Road (Dudley Road and Bearwood). Between the hours of midnight and 05.00 on 24, 25 and 27 March, everyone travelling out from or in to the City on these roads, by taxicab, bicycle or on foot is counted. Overall 2,389 people are seen, 1,614 leaving the City, and 775 entering, the majority of whom (82%) did so on a bicycle. On the basis of these figures, the Committee decides that it would not be justified in establishing the suggested night service.

31 March — The first figures for the Bristol Road motor omnibus service show:

- Receipts (per car mile)   12.375d
- Expenditure (per car mile)   9.288d
- Overall receipts   £1,682
- Omnibus depreciation   £1,000
- Interest on capital spent   £175
- Net profit   £507

In addition, it is reported that: 'The effect of running motor omnibuses has been that the road surface has been badly cut up, and no contribution has been made to the cost of road maintenance. This is an important point to the City as a whole, especially as omnibuses are not assessed for rating of permanent way as tramways are.'

31 May — The Hall Green route is extended along the Stratford Road from College Road to Fox Hollies Road.

4 October — The Corporation purchases BMMO's interests within the City. Also acquired are 13 30hp and 17 40hp 34-seater Tilling-Stevens TTA1 and TTA2 double-deck omnibuses, numbered 1-30, and the right to operate the following routes:

2: New Street-Ryland Street-Ivy Bush
3: New Street-Harborne-Queen's Park
4: New Street-Harborne (Duke of York)
7: Corporation Street-Broad Street-Five Ways
9: New Street-Moseley-College Road
10: Ivy Bush-Hockley-Handsworth Wood.

The purchase also includes Tennant Street omnibus garage, which came into use on 25 May 1912 with the commencement of BMMO's Hagley Road and Harborne double-deck motor omnibus services. Only capable of taking 44 single-deck or open-topped double-deck omnibuses, it is used as an omnibus repair works until Tyburn Road Works opens in December 1929.

16 October — Omnibus Route 2 is discontinued as a wartime economy. Various other changes are made to these omnibus routes in their early months, and new services introduced as extensions of the Bristol Road tramway, linking Selly Oak with Northfield and Longbridge.

1915: WARTIME MEASURES

During the year 10 Tilling-Stevens TS3 motor omnibuses chassis are obtained to replace the Daimlers pressed into war service. They are numbered 31-40 and use both the bodies and registration numbers from the impressed vehicles.

Right: Although hybrids, the expedient-led marriage of the Tilling-Stevens TS3 chassis and ex-Daimler bodies produced quite handsome vehicles, as No 37 demonstrates here. These omnibuses seated 16 in the lower saloon and 18 on the open top. *IAL*

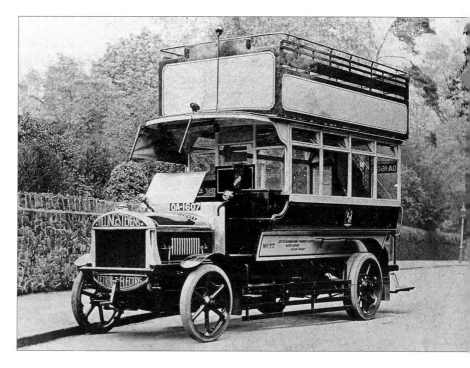

25 January — Route numbers are introduced on tramway services in response to reduced lighting in wartime.

26 March — A long lease is taken on land in Henley Street, Bordesley, close to Kyotts Lake Road Works. This has been used for some years to unload materials brought on the Birmingham & Warwick Canal. A permanent way depot is constructed here and linked to the tramway system.

1 June — The Tramways Committee reports on the effects of 10 months of war. It estimates a loss of traffic of £40,000-£50,000, and is also having to pay allowances to employees on Active Service (estimated at £35,000). In addition, material and labour costs are up, and the Committee has not been able to raise a loan to cover the purchase of BMMO's assets last October. It is forecast that these factors will, cumulatively, absorb the whole of the profits, and the Committee therefore, reluctantly, proposes a fare increase:

- 1d   1 mile 1,200yd
- 1.5d   2 miles 666yd
- 2d   3 miles 393yd
- 2.5d   4 miles 630yd

This is agreed by the Finance Committee, and implemented from 4 July.

12 June — As a further wartime measure, route number stencils are used on tramcar headlights.

1916: New Omnibuses and Routes

During the year a joint conference is held between the Public Works and Tramways committees to consider the effect of motor omnibus traffic and the best means of preventing unnecessary repair work. The committees agree to co-operate, with Tramways giving Public Works at least six months' notice of intended new services. To maintain services, a further 24 motor omnibuses are obtained: 18 Daimler Y and six Tilling-Stevens TS3. The former seat 33 (18/15); the latter chassis are in place of six of the Daimlers, which are commandeered by the War Ministry without entering service. These are numbered 41-58 and will be the Corporation's last omnibus acquisitions before 1922.

2 February — The Acocks Green tramway (Route 44) is opened along Warwick Road to Broad Road.

1 March — Omnibus route changes are implemented, as ex-BMMO services are renumbered:

- 1 — New Street-Five Ways-Moseley (Billesley Lane) (ex-No 9);
- 2 — Ivy Bush-Handsworth Wood (ex-No 10).

1917: Trailer Cars and Shortages

January — Experiments in the use of trailer cars are planned on the Alum Rock and Washwood Heath routes at the behest of Alderman Harrison Barrow, Chairman of the Tramways Committee. These will run from March to June to obtain accurate information on the value of operating trailer cars in the City. The Tramways Committee concludes that it will be necessary for one of the tramway routes to be fully equiped with vehicles of this description. As a result, '301' class tramcars 361, 367, 368, 375 and 379, '401' class tramcar 431, plus ex-CBT bogie cars 451 and 452 are converted to single-deckers in readiness for the experiments, with Nos 28 and 509 becoming the trailers. The trials begin in March, but material shortages lead to their abandonment in May.

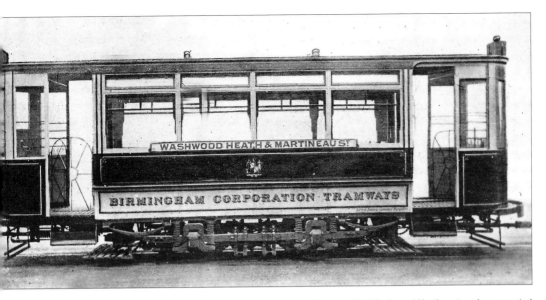

Below: From March to May 1917 the Corporation conducted trailer car experiments on the Washwood Heath route using converted tramcars Nos 451 and 509. Seating 56 and allowing 30 'standees', the vehicles had great potential, but the scheme was scuppered by the shortage of materials in wartime to make the necessary trackwork alterations. These tramcars subsequently worked the Nechells route until 1918. *IAL*

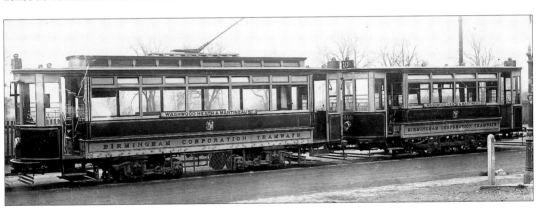

1 May — An acute petrol shortage forces the temporary cessation of omnibus Routes 1-3; this lasts until 1 August.

5 June — Ever rising costs due to the war prompt a further revision of tramway and omnibus fares, but only 'after a good deal of anxious consideration'. Tramway fares are reduced and simplified, with the adoption of a two-mile fare stage for 1d, and the abolition of most return tickets. It is hoped that this will both increase the number of passengers and lighten conductors' duties. On the other hand, omnibus fares are increased to 'meet the greatly increased cost of wages, petrol and other materials'. The new omnibus fare structure is:

- Rednal & Rubery route (from Selly Oak):

Griffins Brook Lane	1d
Northfield (Church Road)	2d
Hawkesley Mill Lane	3d
Longbridge	4d
Rednal or Rubery	5d

- Harborne route (from New Street):

Five Ways	1d
Brook Road	2d
Duke of York	3d
Queen's Park	4d

The Committee also reports on other aspects of the war which are affecting its operations. Between August 1914 and 31 March 1917, 1,620 staff enlisted in HM Forces, of which only 279 have returned, and, sadly, 143 have been killed. There has also been a great increase in the number of women workers, with 1,260 currently employed. Arrangements have also been made to allow wounded soldiers, wearing hospital uniform, to travel free on Corporation tramcars and omnibuses, but at 'busy hours of the day not more than six of the wounded shall travel on one car'.

Top left: Of the 24 omnibuses the Corporation acquired new in 1916, 12 (Nos 41-52) were Daimler 'Y's. No 48 was fitted with a 33 (18/15)-seater Dodson body, and is seen in 1919. Rebodied in 1922, the vehicle was finally withdrawn in 1927. *IAL*

Bottom left: With wartime restrictions eased, the Corporation could look to expanding its services. On 31 March 1919 a new omnibus Route 9 was introduced: New Street-Broad Street-Quinton. Daimler 'Y' No 48 was photographed working the new route. The notice above the Used Ticket box reads: 'PLEASE WAIT UNTIL THE CAR STOPS', showing that tramway thinking still dominated the Department. *IAL*

Right: It wasn't only trams that were converted from double- to single-deckers. In 1919 Tilling-Stevens omnibuses Nos 54-8 received new 25-seater bodies by Brush. No 54 is pictured blocking the road by some allotments in Harborne. *IAL*

1 August — Omnibus route changes and extensions are introduced:

- 1 — New Street-Five Ways-Moseley (Billesley Lane) — resumes, and is extended to Corporation Street and Colmore Row;
- 2 — Ivy Bush-Handsworth Wood — is reinstated.

1918: A Landmark and Major Plans

Birmingham begins an ambitious Arterial Road Scheme to rebuild all of the main City approaches as dual carriageways. This will have major repercussions on the development of tramcar and omnibus services in the City.

4 June — The Tramways Committee reports on a year of 'extreme difficulty' for the Department, in maintaining services at a time of material and staff shortages and increased demand for travelling facilities. This has, at times, only been achieved 'by allowing a considerable level of overcrowding'. Nonetheless, these unprecedented events have allowed the Department to attain a considerable landmark in its history.

For the first time, traffic receipts have exceeded £1 million, and are made up as follows:

- Tramways (198,402,908 passengers) — £984,287
- Omnibuses (764,293 passengers) — £56,809
- Omnibuses for munitions workers — £21,108
- Total — £1,062,204

1919: New Tramcars and Reservations

March — No new tramcars have been ordered since 1913, and, with the War over, public transport in the City is set to expand. Alfred Baker orders another 50 tramcars, similar to the previous batch of six years ago. However, developments in tramway engineering and changes in component suppliers result in the choice of British Thomson-Houston (BTH) electrical equipment, with Dick, Kerr controllers, and bodies by the Brush Electrical Engineering Co Ltd.

31 March — A new omnibus route, 9, is introduced: New Street-Broad Street-Quinton.

15 October — Tramway track in Pebble Mill Road is relaid

on a central reservation, the first of this kind of reserved track in the City. This reconstruction is part of a 'specimen road' trial, in advance of the City's Arterial Road Scheme of dual carriageway building.

1920: NEW ROADS AND TRAMWAYS

During the year, roller-blind route indicators are introduced on the tramcar fleet, and Cotteridge depot is reconstructed and enlarged to hold 40 tramcars, with 32 over pits.

March — The first of the 50 new bogie double-deck tramcars enters service. Numbered 587-636, these again seat 62 (34/28). The last car enters service in March 1921.

13 May — The tramway is extended along Tyburn Road from Gravelly Hill to Holly Lane, all on reserved track, which is the first major length of this construction in the City.

Above: The war had placed restrictions on the ordering of new vehicles, and 50 new tramcars ordered in March 1919,were the first new ones for six years. No 618 from that batch entered service in 1920, and is seen on the extreme right with older cars in Hockley depot. *IAL*

4. 1921-1928: Pioneering Developments

The 1920s saw technical and service developments in Birmingham's tramway and motor omnibus services. Early on came an historic conversion of a worn-out and under-used electric tramway into a trolleybus route, the first of its kind in the country. That the tramway was 'lost' to another form of electric traction 'sweetened the pill' for many, but it would only be repeated once more in the City. Tramcars developed, and 205 new ones were acquired during the eight years in question; the entire fleet gained top covers, newer cars being built totally enclosed. Air brakes were introduced, and speeds increased by the progressive replacement and extension of routes by tracks on dedicated central reservations. Tentacles reached further, to: Lichfield Road, Bordesley Green, Short Heath, Pype Hayes, Hall Green and Stechford, and long smooth runs were created, exemplified by the four extensions that enabled the Bristol Road route to pass through Northfield and Longbridge, *en route* to rural Rednal and Rubery in Worcestershire.

Omnibuses developed too, gaining pneumatic tyres, by order of the Public Works Committee, and top covers. There were 244 new ones, plus some demonstration vehicles, and 13

new routes. Motor omnibuses were also used creatively, not as mere extensions to tramway routes. Termini were brought into the City centre, and imaginative routes were planned and implemented, exploiting the motor omnibus to its greatest advantage in doing things that tramcars could not easily do.

Thus the City's famous Outer and Inner Circle routes were introduced, together with the lesser known City Circle. Cross-City routes were also tried. Supporting infrastructure grew too, as garages were built in Barford Street, Harborne and Acocks Green, so that no longer did omnibuses have to skulk in the dark corners of tramcar depots. Birmingham made motor cars by the thousand, and began to suffer for it as the 'traffic situation' grew worse. Traffic islands were tried, and off-street parking provided, at a price. A trend was set in these

Above: Some parts of Birmingham have changed so much that they are totally unrecognisable today. Brill class No 30 approaches Five Ways along Ladywood Road on a Special working sometime in the early 1920s. The tramcar was never fitted with platform vestibules. *Commercial Postcard/Author's Collection*

Below: A point-duty policeman seems somewhat redundant as a cyclist keeps pace with Corporation tramcar No 11 working the No 6 route from Martineau Street to Perry Barr in the early 1920s. Lewis's massive store boasted 150 departments, two restaurants and a soda fountain. *Commercial Postcard/Author's Collection*

Top right: Starved of new omnibuses until 1922, the Corporation had to 'make-do-and-mend'. That year Tilling-Stevens TS3 No 33, seen in Somerset Road, Edgbaston, received a Dodson body from a Daimler Y vehicle in the 41-49 batch, themselves being rebodied. Like the proverbial 'Irishman's knife', whilst the registration was from the first batch of Daimlers acquired in 1913, neither the chassis nor the body was original. *IAL*

Bottom right: Another seemingly new omnibus which is not all that it appears to be. No 50 was produced in 1922 by putting a new 46 (26/20)-seater Brush K type body on a Daimler Y chassis of 1916. At least it has been emancipated, as the notice above the Used Ticket box now reads: 'WARNING — WAIT UNTIL THE BUS STOPS'. *IAL*

years, one that was reflected in the inclusion of the words 'and Omnibus' in the Tramways Department's name, from 1927.

1921: ALTERNATIVES TO TRAMWAYS

19 July — The Tramways Committee has been reviewing the condition of the Nechells route (opened 1 January 1907). A report shows that the track is worn out, and that the line carries fewer passengers than most. Reinstatement of the track is estimated at £90,000, set against traffic receipts for the route in 1920 of £28,300, which produced an overall deficit of £3,340. Alternatives are sought, and an experiment with 'railless trolley vehicles' is recommended. This would allow the existing tramway feeder and overhead to be retained, only requiring their alteration (estimated at £3,000), and road resurfacing after track removal (estimated at £15,000). With the purchase of 12 new trolleybuses (estimated at £36,000), this option appears to save £36,000 over the upgrading of the infrastructure of an under-used tramway route, and frees 12 tramcars (nominal value £18,000) for use elsewhere on the system. The Ministry of Transport has been consulted on the matter and has consented to the conversion. Services are expected to start in April or May 1922.

Below: Birmingham Corporation made history on 27 November 1922 when trolleybuses were substituted for tramcars on the Nechells route; the first trolleybus-for-tram route conversion in the UK, and the first in the world to use double-deck top-covered vehicles. To inaugurate the service 12 Railless vehicles (Nos 1-12) were acquired with 51 (25/26)-seater bodies by Charles Roe of Leeds. This is No 6 outside Washwood Heath depot, from where the service was operated. *National Motor Museum*

Right: A front three-quarter view of Corporation trolleybus No 6 outside Washwood Heath depot, showing its very tramcar-like appearance. The trolleybuses used the single tramway overhead wire, and made a current return through a metal skate, positioned in one of the tram rails which was dragged along behind the vehicle. *National Motor Museum*

September — The Corporation orders 12 double-deck trolleybuses from Railless Ltd, with bodies by Charles H. Roe Ltd.

9 November — The City terminus of tram Routes 13 (High Street-Small Heath) and 15 (High Street-Yardley) is transferred to Dale End.

1922: AN HISTORIC CONVERSION

Birmingham's Public Works Committee is reluctant to agree to the introduction of motor omnibus services, owing to the damage these cause to road surfaces. It insists on its prior approval before new services are introduced. In response the Tramways Committee cites the case of a free 'omnibus' service, in the form of a motor lorry being run daily from a public house in Harborne to a private garage in Bartley Green, against which no action can be taken as fares are not charged. The year also sees the purchase of 12 K-type double-deck omnibus bodies from Brush, which are mounted on existing Daimler chassis from the batch acquired in 1916.

14 August — The Nechells tramway service is withdrawn between Nechells Green and the Cuckoo Bridge Terminus, and replaced by a temporary omnibus service whilst the track is lifted and the road surface made good in readiness for the introduction of trolleybuses.

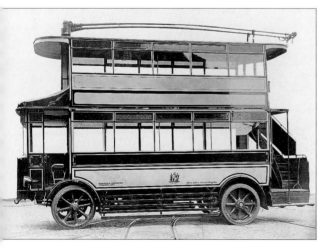

Left: Birmingham Corporation's first postwar omnibus was No 59, an AEC 503 fitted with a 54-seater (28/36) Fry body. This was purchased in 1922 after a month's trial as a demonstrator, It is seen in Harborne on the 4 service from New Street. *IAL*

Below left: The lower saloon of Birmingham Corporation's first postwar omnibus No 59, showing the padded and upholstered seat cushions and a fare schedule for the services to Rednal, Rubery, Moseley, Harborne, Quinton and Handsworth Wood. *IAL*

Above: The delivery of new omnibuses allowed the development of new services in the outer suburbs, including the Outer Circle (11) Route, the second section of which, between Erdington and Acocks Green, opened on 15 June 1923. For more lightly-used services eight Leyland A1s were acquired, with 20-seater bodies by local maker John Buckingham Ltd. *IAL*

Below: The success of the outer suburban omnibus services led the Corporation to acquire more low-capacity single-deckers which suited one-man operation. In 1923 eight Daimler CK2s were bought, each fitted with a 24-seater body by Strachan & Brown of London. Here are six of the batch at the Daimler works prior to delivery. *IAL*

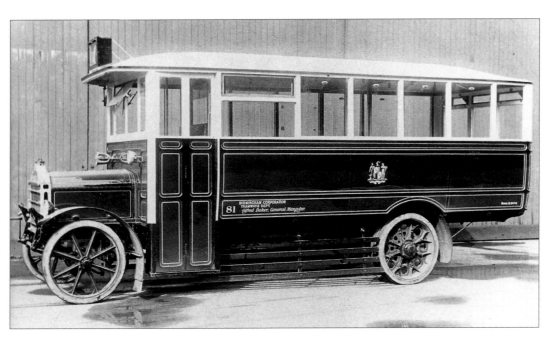

17 *September* — The section of the Lichfield Road between Aston Hall Road and Salford Bridge is reopened as a dual carriageway with the tramway on a central reservation, the latest in the City's Arterial Road Scheme programme.

9 *October* — The Acocks Green tramway route is extended down the Warwick Road to Westley Road, in the centre of Acocks Green.

26 *November* — Nechells tram Route 7 officially closes.

27 *November* — Trolleybuses are substituted on the Nechells route; this is the first trolleybus-for-tram route conversion in the UK, and the first in the world to use double-deck top-covered vehicles. Trolleybuses work between Old Square and Nechells, a distance of 2 miles 772yd, and operate from Washwood Heath tramcar depot. Movement between this depot and the route requires travelling along a tramway route not converted to trolleybus operation. The trolleybuses use the single tramway overhead wire, and effect a circuit return through a metal skate, positioned in one of the tram rails and dragged along behind the vehicle.

1923: BRISTOL ROAD TRAMWAY EXTENSIONS

The Public Works Committee agrees to a number of omnibus service extensions, but only after stipulating that the buses must be fitted with pneumatic tyres. The Corporation also adopts top covers for all its double-deck omnibuses, becoming the first transport operator to do so. It also adds 14 AEC 503 open-top double-deck omnibuses to the fleet. These are numbered 60-71, 89 and 90, having 54-seater bodies by Brush (28/26); nine Daimler CK2 single-deckers are also acquired, numbered 80-88, one with a 21-seater body, the rest seating 24.

8 *January* — The first section of what will later become the Outer Circle (No 11) omnibus route is opened: King's Heath-

Above: A close-up of Daimler CK2 No 81 at the Daimler factory. Although delivered with solid tyres, these were soon changed for pneumatics. *IAL*

Below: A detail of Daimler CK2 No 82 after it was fitted with pneumatic tyres. The prominent horn is a striking feature. *IAL*

Hagley Road, via Cotteridge, Selly Oak and Harborne. It is numbered 10 at this stage, and is operated by eight Leyland A1 20-seater single-deckers, worked by the drivers only.

15 January — Washwood Heath depot accepts omnibuses as well as tramcars and trolleybuses, but loses this allocation from 25 October 1925. Omnibus Route 11 is also inaugurated: Acocks Green-Yardley-Erdington (Six Ways); this is later incorporated with Route 10 to form the Outer Circle.

29 January — Omnibus Route 12 introduced: Harborne (Duke of York)-Bartley Green; from 14 April 1926 it is rerouted to run from the City centre.

February — A decision is made to put top covers on all the remaining open-topped tramcars. The work is undertaken at Kyotts Lake Road Works and completed by 1925.

31 March — During the 18 weeks that the trolleybus service has been operating on the former Nechells tramway route £8,811 has been received in receipts, and expenses of £5,788 incurred, leaving a gross profit of £3,023. These figures are taken as indicating 'the successful inauguration of the Trolley Omnibus system in the City'.

1 April — A City centre loop omnibus service commences. Harborne and Moseley services operate around the City centre via Corporation Street, Bull Street and Colmore Row, and are worked by alternate vehicles in each direction.

2 April — Omnibus Route 2 is extended to Five Ways and New Street.

April-May — Still more tramcars are needed for the growing Bristol Road tramway and a proposed fare reduction. Accordingly, 25 more cars very similar to Nos 587-636 are ordered. The competitive nature of the component supply market at this time makes the choice of contractor all the harder. A number of companies are involved in the supply of the electrical and mechanical items, but the bodies are all built by the Midland Railway Carriage & Wagon Co Ltd at Washwood Heath.

26 May — A through tramway service commences to Bilston from Colmore Row, worked jointly with the South Staffordshire Tramways (Lessee) Co. Alternate tramcars work through to Bilston Town Hall. This arrangement lasts until 31 March 1924.

5 June — The Tramways Committee reports on the urgent need for 'additional car shed accommodation'. A review of the depots affected shows the extent of the overcrowding:

Depot	Over pits	Total cars	Railless/'buses
Miller Street	45	62	
Perry Barr	20	20	
Witton	24	33	
Washwood Heath	38	38	16
Rosebery Street	54	77	

Although this shows Rosebery Street to be the most seriously overcrowded depot, it is decided that the Miller Street site offers the greatest potential for extension and remodelling. A scheme to achieve this is drawn up by Alfred Baker, to provide for the accommodation of 102 tramcars, with 95 of these being over pits, and for the centralisation of the Permanent Way Department at the depot. In detail, this

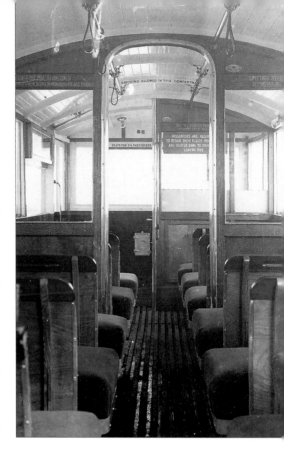

Above: The interior of Daimler CK2 No 82. The front section was for smokers, who were requested not to occupy those seats behind the glass screen 'WHEN OTHERS ARE VACANT'. *IAL*

envisages: 'The extension of the existing car shed to provide accommodation for 25 additional cars; the erection of a new bay to accommodate 25 more cars; the provision of new offices, men's paying-in room, mess rooms, general stores, lavatories, etc; and also the erection of new assembly and recreation rooms for employees.' The work is costed at £30,000, and one of the ideas behind it is to allow Perry Barr depot to be closed and reworked as an omnibus garage.

15 June — The second section of the future Outer Circle (11) route is opened between Erdington and Acocks Green.

July — In recognition of the great changes in the operations of the Tramways Department since its foundation 20 years earlier, new *Bye-laws and Regulations* are drafted and adopted by the Council. These specifically address the operation of motor omnibuses and trolleybuses, not part of the projected Tramways service when the original *Bye-laws and Regulations* were adopted in 1903.

August — A three-month trial begins with a single-deck trolleybus on the Nechells route. It is temporarily given the number 13 in the fleet. The trial lasts until October.

Right: By comparison with the Corporation's new tramcars, and especially its new omnibuses, the standard of comfort offered by the older vehicles paled. This was especially so in the case of the former CBT tramcars, such as No 486, seen in the yard at Kyotts Lake Road Works before being reconstructed in 1923/4. *Author's Collection*

Below: Following its reconstruction, No 486 was to all outward appearances a Corporation tramcar. Despite this, and a series of equipment modifications as late as 1933, the ex-CBT cars fell below the standard offered by the true Corporation vehicles. Once route abandonments created surplus rolling stock, their withdrawal began, although No 486 lasted until March 1939. *IAL*

Top left: Whilst the Corporation's omnibuses offered upholstered seats, even new tramcars, such as '637' class No 640 of 1923, had longitudinal wooden seats when new. These were replaced with upholstered tilting seats during 1927. *IAL*

Below left: Creature comforts were few and far between for tramcar and omnibus drivers, and even when the former were treated to platform vestibules, the latter were still exposed to the elements. A change came c1923 when rebodied Daimler Y No 48 was fitted with an experimental windscreen. *IAL*

Top right: The Corporation's trolleybus fleet was bolstered in 1924 with the delivery of No 13. This was an EMB vehicle, with a Low-Step 48 (28/20)-seater body by English Electric, who also supplied the electrical equipment. Seen outside Washwood Heath depot, No 13 was in service only until 1926. *IAL*

Bottom right: This rear three-quarter view shows the low step on trolleybus No 13 to good advantage. *EMB6/IAL*

1 October — An extension of the Bristol Road tramway to Northfield is opened as Route 69, and runs mainly on reserved track.

October — The first of the new batch of 25 bogie double-deck tramcars enters service after assembly at Hockley depot. Numbered 637-661, these have totally-enclosed upper decks, which give a slight increase in seating capacity to 63 (35/28). They are the first totally-enclosed tramcars in Birmingham, the last of the batch entering service in January 1924. In October a further order for 20 similar tramcars is placed, again using a variety of contractors, but this time having bodies by the Brush Electrical Engineering Co Ltd.

6 November — Omnibus Route 13 is introduced: Stratford Road-Stoney Lane-Yardley Wood. From 1 October 1925 this starts from the City centre.

17 December — The Bristol Road tramway is extended to Longbridge as Route 72, running entirely on reserved track, save for that portion through Northfield.

1924: BLACK COUNTRY ROUTES

Land is leased in Sampson Road, Bordesley, close to Kyotts Lake Road, and a paint shop erected there which can accommodate 32 tramcars. This opens in 1925, and is used until the late 1930s, when the declining tramcar fleet renders it surplus to requirements. A further 31 AEC 504 double-deck omnibuses are also delivered; 30 have 52-seater (26/26) bodies by Shorts, the other has a special 50-seater body by Brush; these are numbered 101-131.

March-April — The 20 tramcars ordered in October 1923 enter service after assembly at Hockley depot. Numbered 662-681, they again seat 63 (35/28)

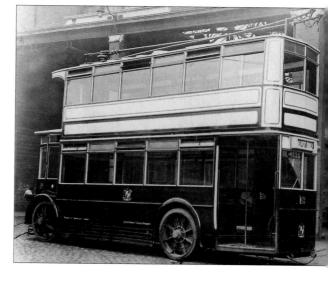

31 March — The South Staffordshire Tramways (Lessee) Co's lease on Albion depot expires, and this reverts to Birmingham Corporation, which closes it on 1 April. Subsequently it is only used to stable tramcars during football matches at The Hawthorns.

31 March — End-of-year figures provide details of the first full year's operation of the trolleybus service on the former Nechells tramway route. The total receipts are £25,420 and operating costs £17,183, giving a gross profit of £8,237.

Top left: The most glaring difference between Birmingham Corporation's tramcars and omnibuses was in the provision of top covers for upper deck passengers: trams had them, buses didn't. In 1924 AEC 503 No 62 was fitted with an experimental top cover for evaluation purposes. Although it did not run in service, this paved the way for future developments. *IAL*

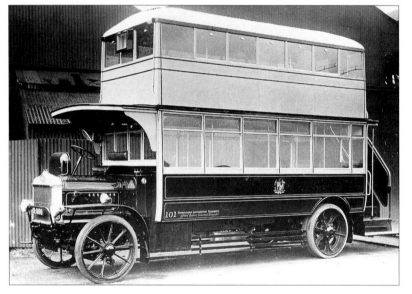

Centre left: On 24 July 1924 Birmingham Corporation scored another UK first by placing into service a top-covered double-deck omnibus. Designed by the General Manager, Alfred Baker, it was based upon an AEC 504 chassis and numbered 101 in the fleet. The vehicle was photographed at the Brush works, where its 50 (26/24)-seater body was built. *Passenger Transport Journal/IAL*

Bottom left: Thirty production top-covered AEC 504 vehicles were delivered in 1924. They had 52 (26/26)-seater bodies by Short Bros, differing also from No 101 by having a peak over the top-deck windows. No 105 is posed with open-topped AEC 503 No 62 in Somerset Road, Edgbaston. *IAL*

Right: Covered the top decks of the AEC 504s may have been, but they offered a spartan level of comfort, with wooden seats and stern warnings against smoking. *Passenger Transport Journal/IAL*

Below right: After rebuilding in 1924 the ex-CBT tramcars, such as No 499 (ex-247), closely resembled the Corporation-designed vehicles. Thus given a new lease of life, No 499 remained in service until January 1937. *Passenger Transport Journal/IAL*

Right: The tell-tale difference between the ex-CBT tramcars and most Corporation-designed ones was the lack of the characteristic half-hexagonal dash, shown here on No 492 (ex-231). The rebuilding was worthwhile as the car gave a further 15 years' service. *IAL*

Below right: April 1924 saw the Corporation take responsibility for the West Bromwich routes and the extension of the Bristol Road route to Rednal. An extra 40 tramcars were acquired for these duties, ordered in two batches of 20. The last of the first batch was No 681, which entered service that month. This is a close-up of its platform equipment. *Modern Transport/IAL*

April — With the takeover of the West Bromwich routes, and a further extension to the Bristol Road route imminent, Alfred Baker adds a further 20 tramcars to the batch ordered in October 1923.

1 April — Birmingham Corporation takes over the running of tramways in West Bromwich. It introduces a through service to Dudley (74), plus one to Wednesbury (75). Tram Route 23 (Colmore Row-Handsworth) becomes a short working of these routes. The initial approach for this came from West Bromwich Corporation during 1923, and it was agreed that Birmingham Corporation would operate these services on the basis of being paid the whole of their operating expenses, the receipts from the West Bromwich lines being paid to that Corporation.

14 April — The Bristol Road tramway is extended to Rednal (Route 70) on reserved track.

24 July — A top-covered double-deck omnibus, designed by Alfred Baker, is put into service. It is based upon an AEC 504 chassis and is numbered 101 in the fleet. This is claimed at the time to be the first modern top-covered omnibus to operate in the UK. Birmingham Corporation did not order any more open-topped double-deckers after this date.

3 October — Birchfield Road depot, which had reopened c1914, is closed for conversion to an omnibus garage.

December — The first of the 20 additional tramcars ordered in April enters service following assembly at Hockley depot. Numbered 682-701, they seat 63 (35/28). The last of the batch enters service in February 1925.

15 December — Tramway extension omnibus Route 15 is introduced: Coventry Road-Stechford.

1925: SINGLE-DECK TRAMCARS?

A further 40 AEC 504 type omnibuses are obtained, in batches of 30 and 10. All have 52-seater bodies by Shorts (26/26); they are numbered 132-171.

7 January — Birchfield Road tramcar depot reopens as a temporary omnibus garage, but closes on 10 June with the opening of Barford Street omnibus garage, to be converted and extended, reopening on 28 October for omnibuses. A new omnibus service (16) also begins: City-Hockley-Handsworth Wood.

March — Still more tramcars are needed, and Alfred Baker recommends that 30 bogie double-deckers be ordered. Again, a variety of contractors is used, but, save for motors being from the General Electric Co Ltd, they are the same suppliers patronised for the previous batch of cars.

Above: The Short Bros-bodied AEC 504s proved very successful and a further 40 entered service in 1925, including No 152, seen here at the foot of Stonehouse Hill, near the end of the Lapal canal tunnel in California. *Passenger Transport Journal/IAL*

Right: A significant difference to both the ride and appearance of the AEC 504s was made when they were fitted with pneumatic tyres. Compare this shot of No 163 of 1925 with the one of No 152. *Passenger Transport Journal/IAL*

10 June — Barford Street omnibus garage opens. A converted factory, this causes the Department considerable problems in its early years owing to the large numbers of children who congregate near its entrances. Petitions are received from the residents of Barford and Banacre Streets on the subject, but by 5 July 1927 the Tramways Committee is able to report that the 'interest of the children has diminished recently, and the omnibuses do not now attract so much attention'. Clearly the novelty wears off.

16 June — The Tramways Committee reports on a detailed study it has made into the advantages and disadvantages of single-deck tramcar operation in the City. The advantages are seen as being in the areas of:

- *Safety* — less likely to overturn;
- *Passenger accidents* — lessened, as the Conductor is always on the same deck and can supervise passengers boarding and leaving the car at all times;
- *Time schedules* — improved, as time spent at stops is reduced and loading can be improved by the adoption of a rear platform entry, front platform exit passenger flow; and
- *Operating costs* — reduced, as the cars are lighter, causing less wear on the track, and, lacking top decks, have less bodywork to maintain, which is also under less stress without the weight of an upper deck bearing down upon it.

The disadvantages of single-deck tramcars are seen as:

- *Capacity* — single-deck tramcars the same length as the latest double-deck cars (33ft 6in) could only seat about 30. The Continental practice, of providing longer platforms for standing passengers, is a possibility, but it is felt unlikely to be permitted in Birmingham. 'In addition, it is only reasonable that people going to and from work should be provided with seats and not be compelled to stand upon the platforms';
- *Smoking* — would have to be prohibited altogether, or permitted inside the cars, which would be objectionable to a great number of passengers;

- *Depot space* — would be seriously overtaxed as more single-deck tramcars would be required to provide the seating accommodation of double-deck cars;
- *Additional staff* — more trams would require more staff to operate and maintain them, leading to increased operating costs.

Responding to a suggestion that a trial of single-deck tramcars be instituted on the Rednal route, the Tramways Committee reports that: 'The number of cars normally running on this route is between 40 and 50. On fine Saturday afternoons and Sundays during the summer months, and on Bank Holidays, a very large number of cars have to be drafted from other routes to deal with the traffic to the Lickey Hills.' These extra cars would have to be double-deckers, and would therefore slow the service down. 'On August Bank Holiday last year (1924) no less than a half-minute service of cars was required to accommodate the crowds travelling to and from the Lickeys …carrying on average over 60 passengers each.' Single-deck tramcars, carrying only 30 passengers each, would dictate a quarter-of-a-minute service interval — impossible to maintain. The use of trailer cars has again been advocated as part of this trial of single-deck cars. Drawing upon the experience with these in the previous decade it is commented that 'this would not appear to be a satisfactory solution, having regard to the narrow and tortuous streets of the City and the traffic congestion therein', especially as 'a car and trailer totalling over 67ft in length would have to be employed'. The net effect of these deliberations is that the Tramways Committee cannot recommend the Council to experiment with single-deck tramcars.

September — The first of the 30 tramcars ordered in March enters service after being assembled at Moseley Road depot. Numbered 702-731, they feature more upholstered seating than previous cars, which reduces their capacity to 60 (33 upper saloon, 27 lower). The last of these cars enters service in January 1926.

14 October — The tramway is extended from College Road to Pelham Road, Alum Rock. This is the only extension not to be built on reserved track.

4 November — The tramway is extended from Bordesley Green to Bordesley Green East.

1926: THE TIDE TURNS

Other road traffic is giving the City Council problems, and the first gyratory traffic island is introduced at Six Ways, Erdington, as a means of traffic control at busy intersections. The Council also establishes a Joint Traffic Committee, made up of representatives from the Public Works, Town Planning, Watch and Tramways Committees, plus the Lord Mayor, Deputy Mayor, Town Clerk, and respective Committee Chief Officers. This will produce proposals which will have repercussions for both tramway and omnibus operations. Meanwhile, 36 more AEC 504 double-deck omnibuses are delivered. They have 52-seater (26/26) bodies by a variety of makers, and are numbered 172-207. The same chassis also forms the basis of a 25-seater, Brush-bodied single-decker, numbered 29. Delivery is also taken of a Guy BKX six-

BIRMINGHAM CORPORATION
TRAMCARS and OMNIBUSES

PROVIDE
EASY FACILITIES FOR REACHING
ALL PARTS OF THE CITY

&

SEE 25 MILES OF
BIRMINGHAM'S SUBURBS
on the
OUTER CIRCLE OMNIBUS
Service No. 11

&

Frequent Services

A. BAKER, *General Manager.*

Above: After 21 years as a public transport operator, Birmingham Corporation had much to be proud of. This was how it promoted itself in the City's Handbook for 1926. Pride of place went to the newly completed Outer Circle service No 11, which was inaugurated on 7 April 1926. *Author's Collection*

wheeler omnibus with a 58-seater body by Shorts (32/26), numbered 208. Three more trolleybuses are also purchased from AEC, with 51-seat bodies by Shorts, numbered 14-16.

January — An order for 30 more tramcars is placed with the English Electric Co Ltd, with bodies by Brush, and bogies by the Electro-Mechanical Brake Co Ltd (EMB). These tramcars will also feature air brakes.

8 February — A branch from Bristol Road tramway to Rubery is opened as Route 71, running on reserved track.

26 February — Omnibus Route 8, Saltley-Small Heath-Stratford Road, is introduced; this forms the first part of the Inner Circle route, eventually completed on 8 February 1928.

March — Tramcar No 706 of the latest batch is used for trials of an air-brake system produced by the Westinghouse Brake & Signal Co Ltd. This ultimately proves problematic, and is removed in April 1928.

31 March — End-of-year figures show the best Tramways revenue performance of recent years, with an additional one

Above: A further 36 AEC 504s entered service with the Corporation in 1926, 10 of which (Nos 192-201) had 52 (26/26)-seater bodies by Thompson & Co of Louth in Lincolnshire. This view shows No 193 at the bodymakers prior to delivery to Birmingham.
Lance Brown/IAL

Below: A clearer view of the lines of one of the Thompson-bodied AEC 504s is gained from this shot of No 198 after it had been fitted with pneumatic tyres. *IAL*

Above: Viewed from St Martin's Church, the Bull Ring is a hive of activity c1926 as a Corporation tramcar swings out of Moor Street working Route 17 High Street-Hall Green. In the foreground a pair of Midland Red omnibuses have parked up, while the indoor and outdoor markets are doing a roaring trade.
Commercial Postcard/ Author's Collection

Left: A branch from the Bristol Road tramway opened to Rubery on 8 February 1926 as Route 71, running on reserved track. Like the extension to Rednal opened the year before, this was in a rural setting, right on the çity boundary with Worcestershire.
Commercial Postcard/ Author's Collection

Official 1926 Edition. (Nineteenth Year)

BIRMINGHAM

T.O.S.

(TRAM, OMNIBUS & STREET)

GUIDE

3ᵈ   3ᵈ

INCLUDING MAP, COMPLETE STREET DIRECTORY, & PLACES OF INTEREST.
Showing at a glance where each Tram and 'Bus starts from, which to take, where to get off, and Right or Left Turn to take for Road or Street required.

If you are Seeking a House —

The Wesleyan & General Assurance Society offers a unique house-purchase scheme, whereby eight-tenths of the value is advanced on Freehold, or three-fourths on Leasehold ; and an Endowment Policy is included which transfers the house to your dependant should you die before repayment, free of further cost.   Call or write for full details.

WESLEYAN & GENERAL
ASSURANCE SOCIETY

Chief Office   A·L·Hunt
Steelhouse Lane   F.S.S, F.C.I.I
Birmingham.   General Manager

Left: Since 1907 practical help in the form of the *Birmingham Tram, Omnibus & Street Guide* had been available to the citizen of or visitor to the City; this is the cover to the 1926 edition. Whilst the AEC 504 at right is passable, goodness knows what the tramcar at left is meant to be!
Author's Collection

Below: With the sole exception of EMB trolleybus No 13, the original 12 Railless vehicles had a monopoly on the Nechells route for its first four years. In 1926 No 10 is seen waiting in Old Square in a view which emphasises the height of these vehicles. *R. B. Parr/IAL*

million miles run and 11 million passengers carried over previous records.

7 April — Omnibus route 1A is introduced as an extension of the 1 to Acocks Green. The 25-mile Outer Circle omnibus Route 11, the first of three Circle routes, is also completed. It operates at a 3-4 mile radius from the City centre.

7 June — A new omnibus Route 5, City-Witton-Perry Common (College Road), is introduced. It uses the number of the former Longbridge-Rednal tramway extension service, last run on 14 April 1924.

23 June — The tramway is extended from Stockland Green to Short Heath on reserved track. Route 1 becomes a short working of Route 78.

6 July — The Tramways Committee reports, prophetically, that its members 'have under consideration the further extension of omnibus services in various parts of the City, and are now engaged in preparation of plans, etc, for the erection of suitable garages, being of the opinion that in all probability

Left: Assistance was at hand in the form of three AEC 604 trolleybuses, Nos 14-16, which were acquired in 1926. The 51 (25/26)-seater bodies were by Short Bros; exemplified by No 15 these, resembled the Roe bodies on the Railless vehicles, but were deeper and more rounded at the front. *Passenger Transport Journal/IAL*

Below: Also acquired in 1926 was an AEC 607 trolleybus with a 52 (26/26)-seater body by Vickers. Given the fleet number 17, this is seen in Old Square in May 1930. *G. H. F. Atkins*

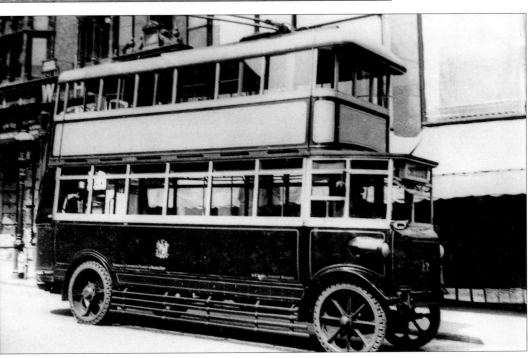

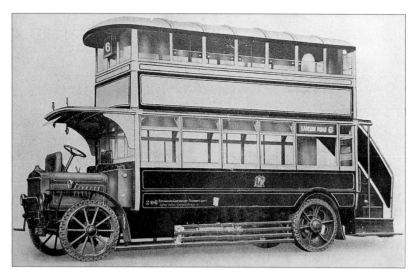

future transport developments in the City, with perhaps some short extensions of tramways, will lie with this system of transport'. At the same time, 'short extensions of tramways' are being planned along reserved tracks in the Tyburn Road, and in the Stechford and Hall Green areas. To save time and cost, powers for these are to be secured by the promotion of a Light Railways Order.

August — In an equally prophetic move, the Tramways Department obtains authorisation to purchase a £315 12hp Austin two-seater all-weather car for the use of the staff, 'owing to the wide extension of the Department's activities'.

4 August — The General Manager of the Tramways Department, Alfred Baker, attains 65 years on this date and should retire unless the Council directs otherwise. In view of his high standing in the Public Transport profession and his

close involvement with planned tramway extensions and the development of omnibus services, the Tramways Committee recommends the retention of Mr Baker's services for a further period of one year, which the Council endorses.

September — The first of the latest batch of 30 tramcars enters service. Numbered 732-761, they are the first Birmingham trams to feature air brakes from new. They also have blue leather upholstery, which gives a seating capacity of 63 (35/28). Assembled at Coventry Road depot, the last of the cars enters service in March 1927.

29 September — A new omnibus service, City-Sandon Road (Bearwood), is introduced. It is given the number 6, formerly allocated to the Rubery tramway extension service last run on 7 February.

12 October — Harborne omnibus garage is opened, with a

capacity for 100 vehicles. Tennant Street garage (ex-BMMO) closes as an operational garage on the same day, but remains open for repair work.

11 November — A portion of the Bristol Road tramway, repositioned on a central reservation between Pebble Mill Road and Edgbaston Park Road for the construction of a dual carriageway, comes into use.

21 November — Omnibus Route 2 is curtailed to start at the Ivy Bush.

1927: FAIRER FARES

A site is purchased on Tyburn Road for a new omnibus overhaul and repair works. The Corporation also places its first large order for motor omnibuses: 76 AEC 507s, with double-deck bodies by a variety of makers, but mostly Shorts, numbered 210-285. Nos 220-244 have special low-height 46-seater bodies by Shorts, which feature an unusual 'herringbone' 26-seat arrangement on the upper deck; these are for use on the Inner Circle route. A second six-wheeled

double-decker, a Karrier DD6 with a 60-seater body by Shorts (32/28), is also acquired and numbered 209.

21 February — An extension of the Tyburn Road tramway to Pipe Hayes opens along reserved track, built at a cost of £26,470.

1 March — The Joint Traffic Control Committee reports. Its Traffic Control Policy recommends the provision of parking places for cars both on and off the highway, plus alterations to tramway and omnibus services to facilitate traffic flow, and suggestions for one-way streets. These take two or three years to come into effect.

11 April — The latest time for the issue of Workmen's Return Tickets is put back from 08.00 to cater for those who can complete their journey by 09.00. This concession is estimated to cost the Department £37,000 in the financial year 1927/8.

5 July — The Tramways Committee reports back to the Council on the advisability of a general reduction in tram and omnibus fares. It cites the concession on Workmen's Return fares instigated on 11 April, but notes that its finances do not

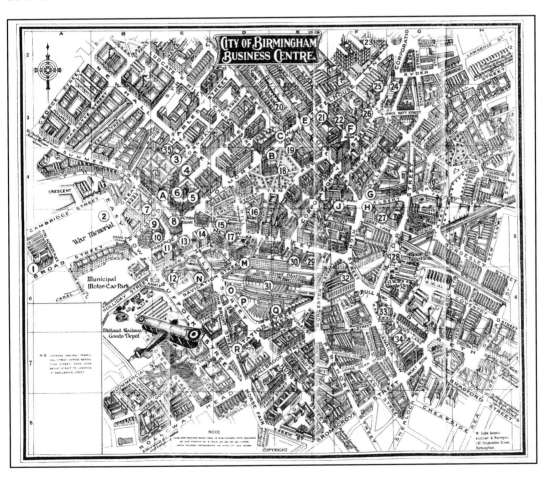

Above: Birmingham Chamber of Commerce commissioned this isometric view of the City centre for use in its annual publications. For those who do not remember the City as it was, this is an invaluable guide. The numbers are important buildings and the letters denote the tramway termini. *Author's Collection*

EDGE | 6"X 12" KERB | 4"X 6" SETT | ON 6" CONCRETE | 4" TARRED MACADAM | 8" SLAG PITCHING | 6" ASHES | TURF ON 3" SOIL | 3" RED ASHES | B.S.S.RAIL N°8 112·9 LBS PER YD | 2" BALLAST | 7"X 9"X 4½" CREOSOTED DEAL SLEEPER | 6" EARTHENWARE PIPE | 6 TO 7" SLAG PITCHING | 6" ASHES | 3" GRAVEL ON 4" ASHES | 6"X 12" KERB | 4"X 6" SETT | ON 6" CONCRETE | ← 1 IN 30 | BEDDIN

Above: The details of how the Corporation reconstructed its arterial road to accommodate central tramway reservations are revealed in this illustration from the City's Handbook for 1927. It shows a portion of the Bristol Road, looking towards the City from the vicinity of Edgbaston Park Road. *Author's Collection*

Left: The Corporation opened an extension of the Tyburn Road tramway to Pipe Hayes, along reserved track, on 21 February 1927; this had been built at a cost of £26,470. The terminus arrangements are seen here with tramcar No 688. *Commercial Postcard/ Author's Collection*

Left: Selly Oak tramway & omnibus depot was formally opened by the Lord Mayor on 8 July 1927. It was one of the largest and best-appointed in the country, being 280ft long and 186ft wide, and holding 80 tramcars and omnibuses. This view shows the tramcar roads and bus standings. *The Electric Railway & Tramway Journal/IAL*

Right: The front entrance to Selly Oak depot at its opening. Within a few years, improvements to Harborne Lane greatly altered the depot approaches. Designed by F. J. Hopkins, Building Superintendent of the Tramways Department, the depot cost £37,000. *The Electric Railway & Tramway Journal/IAL*

Below: AEC and Daimler linked up in 1927, and the majority of new 'buses ordered that year were delivered as Associated Daimlers (ADC). One such was No 257, an ADC 507 with a 52 (26/26)-seater body by Short Bros. This incorporated new features, such as an enclosed cab and a roof mounted destination box. *IAL*

permit further reductions. Were these possible, first consideration would be given to the large number of people who are compelled to reside long distances away from their work.

8 July — A new tramway depot is formally opened at Harborne Lane, Selly Oak. It is one of the largest and best-appointed in the country, and has cost £37,000. The work of F. J. Hopkins, Building Superintendent of the Tramways Department, the depot is 280ft long and 186ft wide, and holds 80 tramcars and omnibuses; it comes into use on 12 July, when Dawlish Road depot, Bournbrook, closes.

4 August — The tenure of Alfred Baker as General Manager of the Tramways Department is further extended by the Council for one year, at the end of which Mr Baker 'has expressed a desire that he should be allowed to retire'.

26 September — Birmingham's first cross-City motor omnibus service is introduced between Perry Common and Portland Road, numbered 7 in this direction and 5 in the reverse.

18 October — The Department's name is changed to 'Birmingham Corporation Tramways & Omnibus Department', to reflect the growing number of motor omnibus services it is operating.

1928: KEEPING IT IN THE FAMILY

Such are Birmingham's traffic problems that the City opens its first off-street car park on the site of the former Old Wharf Canal basin and offices (demolished in 1913), between Easy Row and Bridge Street. It has spaces for 750 cars. Charges are 1s for any of three 7-8 hour periods, or 1s 6d all day. Omnibus routes formerly terminating at tram termini are also brought into the City centre, and another 52 AEC 507 double-deck omnibuses are delivered. Ten, numbered 286-295, have low-height bodies by Shorts, with the same herringbone pattern of upper-deck seating as on Nos 220-244 in 1927; the remainder, numbered 296-337, have 50-seat bodies by Shorts (26/24).

January-February — With the impending takeover of the Dudley and Oldbury via Smethwick routes, Alfred Baker recommends the purchase of 50 more tramcars. These are to have English Electric equipment and Brush bodies, as before.

6 February — A second cross-City motor omnibus service is introduced: Hall Green-Kingstanding, numbered 29.

7 February — A petition is presented to the Council concerning the noise made by tramcars negotiating the Chapel Lane/Bristol Road junction, which has been in use for a little over six months. The problem is caused by the tramcar wheels squealing on the curve, and the Tramways Committee authorises the provision of water sprinklers to lubricate this, which solves the problem.

8 February — The Inner Circle, the second of the three Circle omnibus routes, commences, running at a radius of around 1½-2 miles from the City centre.

29 February — Alfred Baker retires and is replaced by his son, Arthur Chantrey Baker. At its March meeting the Tramways & Omnibus Committee passes a resolution charting and commending Mr Baker's 24 years' service to the City. His services are to be retained in an advisory capacity until his due retirement date on 3 August. At no point is the obvious relationship between the two Messrs Baker mentioned.

1 March — Arthur Chantrey Baker, the son of Alfred Baker, takes over as General Manager of the Birmingham Corporation Tramways & Omnibus Department. He is 40, and has been with the Department for 20 years, serving as its Chief Engineer since 1920. One of his first duties is to review its tramcar needs, and as a result he recommends the purchase of a further 30 cars, which are needed to operate the Dudley and Oldbury routes to be taken over on 1 April. Initially, cars will be hired from the Birmingham District Power & Traction Co, but these are near life-expired, and just not up to the Corporation's excellent high standard.

19 March — A third cross-City motor omnibus service is introduced: Maypole-Erdington, numbered 17.

April — A further 30 double-deck tramcars are ordered. As before, equipment comes from a variety of suppliers, electrical items being by the General Electric Co, which has a large works at Witton, and the bodies are supplied by Short Bros (Rochester & Bedford) Ltd. The estimated cost of these cars is £65,000. Passing the Council resolution required to

place this order provokes debate concerning the use of direct labour to build some of the tramcars. It is remarked that if this were to take place in buildings especially erected for the purpose it would involve very large expenditure, and, as future transport needs are increasingly to be met by motor omnibuses, the capital outlay could not be justified. An alternative suggestion is the use of Kyotts Lake Road Works for this purpose, but this is also seen as problematic, as the construction of new cars would displace routine maintenance work. Set against either proposal is the added fact that a substantial part of the components making up a tramcar are of such a specialist nature that most would still have to be bought in ready-made from outside manufacturers.

1 April — Birmingham Corporation officially takes over operation of tramways owned by the Birmingham District Power & Traction Co, except the loop in Spon Lane to West Bromwich and Bromford Lane. The Tramways Department commences a tramway service to Oldbury and Dudley via Smethwick. Also acquired is West Smethwick depot, which has covered capacity for 44 tramcars. The tramways operate through the boroughs of Smethwick, Oldbury, Rowley Regis, Tipton and Dudley, and the agreement to work them is effective from 1 January until 31 December 1938.

2 April — The tramway is extended from Highfield Road, Hall Green, to the City boundary near Solihull Cemetery on reserved track, at a cost of £52,919.

June — Acocks Green omnibus garage is opened on Fox Hollies Road; it has capacity for 50 vehicles.

20 June — Selly Oak depot becomes tramcar-only from this date.

3 July — The question of using single-deck tramcars, last reported on by the Tramways Committee on 16 June 1925, has not gone away. In February the Council instructed the Committee to investigate the running of single-deck cars in Bradford. Since March 1927 that Corporation has been conducting experiments with a 39ft 3in, centre-entrance, single-deck tramcar, which carries 60 passengers — 34 seated

Left: The impending takeover of the Dudley and Oldbury via Smethwick routes prompted Alfred Baker to recommend the purchase of 50 extra tramcars. They would be the last he was to order before his retirement on 29 February 1928, and when they entered service they would bear the name of his son, A. C. Baker, as General Manager. No 763 of this batch is seen outside Washwood Heath depot. The cars were the first to have smaller windows on the upper deck.
The Electric Railway & Tramway Journal/IAL

and 26 standing. Also a narrow-gauge tramway (4ft), Bradford has experienced difficulty operating such a long tramcar in its narrow streets. At the time of Birmingham's correspondence on the subject — February to June 1928 — the tramcar is also out of service owing to mechanical problems, which adds weight to Birmingham's decision not to pursue such an experiment itself. (The Bradford car resumes service later in 1928, but is restricted to the almost-straight Stanningley route, and is withdrawn in December 1930.)

26 August — The tramway is extended from Bordesley Green East to Stechford along reserved track, at a cost of £24,124. Route 11 becomes a short working of Route 90 to Stechford via Fazeley Street; Route 12 becomes a short working of Route 84 to Stechford via Deritend.

September — The first of the latest batch of 50 tramcars ordered earlier in the year enters service. Assembled at Moseley Road depot they are numbered 762-811, and seat 62 (35/27). The last of the cars enters service in February 1929.

October — The Corporation approaches Short Bros (Rochester & Bedford) Ltd with a view to having an experimental tramcar constructed with a lightweight body made from aluminium.

1 November — A new omnibus service (30) is introduced: City-Shaftmoor Lane-Oulton Boulevard (Warwick Road).

November — The first of the 30 new tramcars ordered in April enters service. Numbered 812-841, they are assembled at Selly Oak depot. The last car enters service in April 1929.

5. 1929-1935: A Corner Turned

THE COTTERIDGE TERMINUS, KINGS NORTON

As Birmingham entered the 1930s the tramcar reigned supreme as the mass provider of road public transport, but not for long. If one decision could be singled out as signalling a reversal in the City's fiercely pro-tramway policy, it was probably that not to extend the Perry Barr tramway (Route 6) to serve the large new Warren Farm housing development to the north at Kingstanding. How actively this was considered is not clear, but this uncertainty alone speaks volumes. Other cities, with equally fervent housing policies, notably Liverpool, costed tramway extensions into their schemes as a matter of course. Here, and to a lesser extent with the Gospel Lane estate at Fox Hollies, Birmingham chose to meet a new need with a new form of transport: the motor omnibus. Over the seven years in question, this was almost unanimously the

Above: A seemingly redundant point duty policeman encourages car No 816 to the end of the terminus at Cotteridge while 'bus No 329 waits at the Outer Circle stop. The tram is in fact standing just free of the points leading into Cotteridge depot. *Commercial Postcard/Author's Collection*

choice. Little new track was added to the tramway system, and much lost, the period seeing the first abandonments of tramcar routes, with the closure of the Bolton and Hagley Road routes, and those to Lozells and Yardley. The latter were replaced by trolleybuses, but everywhere else the motor omnibus gained ground, with 568 new ones being acquired (diesel engines finding favour), 21 new routes (and many other modifications), plus a massive dedicated overhaul and

75

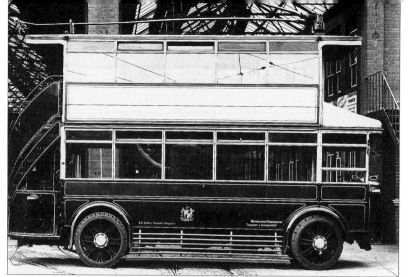

Top left: The means by which trolleybuses gained access to Washwood Heath depot is well illustrated by this shot taken of a Railless vehicle outside the depot in July 1929. Using one trolley boom to collect current from the tramway overhead, the current return was effected through a skate, seen attached to the 'bus at left, which was dragged along in the groove of the tram track. *Passenger Transport Journal/IAL*

Centre left: In the five or six years since the previous view of C orporation Street on page 48 there has been a massive increase in the amount of other traffic which car No 800 has to negotiate as it passes Lewis's department store. *Commercial Postcard/ Author's Collection*

Bottom left: Traffic congestion was less of a problem in the suburbs. On 11 April 1929 car No 525 is seen entering Lozells Road from Wheeler Street on Route 24, and appears to have sounded its gong to alert the man in the foreground of his impending fate. *Commercial Postcard/ Author's Collection*

Top right: Birmingham's last two tramcars both had experimental lightweight aluminium bodies. That for No 842 was built by Short Bros. Equally advanced technically, the car's clean lines were photographed at Rednal terminus in December 1929, just before it entered service. *IAL*

repair facility on the Tyburn Road. In its broader road policy too, the City Council's experiments with traffic signals, one-way systems and traffic islands tacitly favoured the omnibus.

1929: HISTORIC DECISIONS

Birmingham's traffic experiments continue. The first automatic traffic signals in the City are installed at the junctions of Bristol Road/Priory Road and Pershore Road/Priory Road. They are placed on islands in the middle of the carriageway. An extra 40 motor omnibuses are also purchased. Ten are Guy Conquest single-deckers, seating 25, built for one-man operation and numbered 51-60. The rest are AEC Regent double-deckers, all but one having Brush 50-seater bodies (26/24). These are the first Corporation-owned omnibuses to have six-cylinder engines. Numbered 338-367, their design represents a great advance for the period, featuring enclosed staircases, and destination blinds instead of boards.

January — After three months of discussions, the Corporation orders a lightweight tramcar body from Short Bros (Rochester & Bedford) Ltd.

20 March — A new omnibus service (18) commences: King's Norton-Cotteridge-Northfield.

April — Orders are placed with a variety of contractors, including English Electric, for electrical and mechanical equipment for the experimental lightweight-bodied tramcar ordered in January. Learning of the Corporation's interest in lightweight tramcars, the Brush Electrical Engineering Co Ltd makes an approach, and offers to supply a complete tramcar (body and equipment).

May — After due consideration, the Corporation decides to take up the offer made in April by the Brush Electrical Engineering Co Ltd, but only for the lightweight tramcar body. Tenders are sought for the electrical and mechanical equipment.

Right: After also evaluating an ADC 802, a Guy Invincible and a Leyland TD1, Birmingham Corporation decided to place an order for 30 AEC Regents in 1929. No 339 was the second of two delivered with a pre-production prototype chassis, which the manufacturer replaced in 1930. These were the first 'buses in the City's fleet to have enclosed staircases.
Passenger Transport Journal/IAL

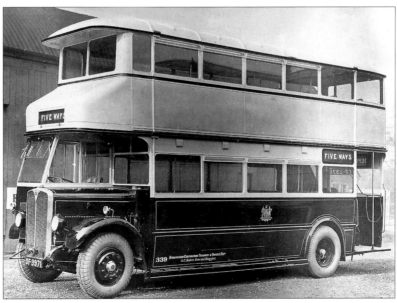

Top left: This view of No 340 shows the lines of the driver's side of Birmingham Corporation's first AEC Regents. The 50 (26/24)-seater Brush bodies had clean lines and incorporated destination blinds. They proved very popular with passengers. *Passenger Transport Journal/IAL*

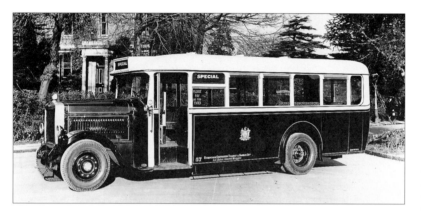

Centre left: The continued expansion of suburban services called for more single-deck 'buses, and in 1929 10 Guy Conquests, Nos 51-60, were delivered. Seating 25, they were built for one-man operation. *Passenger Transport Journal/IAL*

Bottom left: Inside, the Guy Conquests offered high levels of comfort. Smokers were banished to the rear seats, behind the sofa-like benches to the fore here. *Passenger Transport Journal/IAL*

Top right: The investment seen in the tramway and omnibus service was not reflected in the trolleybuses, which were regarded only as an experiment. With only three new vehicles and two demonstrators added to the fleet since 1922, the main burden still rested on the original Railless vehicles, like this one waiting in Old Square in August 1929. *G. H. F. Atkins*

7 May — The Tramways & Omnibus Committee reports to the Council on the condition of the Hagley Road tramway. The Department has estimated that by the end of 1929 this will have 'expended its useful life', and that consideration should be given to its being relaid or replaced. It is reported that the number of passengers using the line has been in decline for several years, and figures are quoted in support:

Year ending	Passengers carried
31 March 1924	9,826,230
31 March 1925	9,804,166
31 March 1926	9,429,989
31 March 1927	6,838,142
31 March 1928	4,993,021
31 March 1929	3,973,922

This decline in passengers is attributed to the operation of omnibus services which travel along the whole or part of Hagley Road:

- Route 9, City centre-Quinton via Broad Street, introduced 31 March 1919;
- Route 6, Sandon Road-City centre, introduced on 29 September 1926;
- Route 5, rerouted to start in Portland Road, Bearwood, and cross the City centre *en route* to Perry Common, from 29 June 1927.

The introduction of the last two services in particular coincides with a steeper decline in the number of tramcar passengers carried, even though neither travels the whole length of the Hagley Road. Passengers' preference for omnibuses is believed to stem from the fact that these services take a direct route into the City, rather than the circuitous one via Holloway Head taken by the tramway. Relaying the track is estimated to cost £44,000, and, given the progressive decline in passengers (which is expected to fall more sharply

with a forthcoming move of the route's City terminus from the Queen's Hotel end of Navigation Street to its Suffolk Street end), an annual loss of over £2,000 is predicted on the route. Motor omnibuses and trolleybuses are both considered for the route, but the latter are discounted because of:

- the quantity of overhead equipment required;
- complications on the Ladywood and Dudley Road tramways; and
- the desirability of not operating two kinds of transport over the same road.

Omnibuses are favoured instead, because:

- the cost of reinstating the road after removal of the tracks will not place its operation by omnibuses at a financial loss; and
- routes can be extended without obtaining special powers, if, for example, there are extensive housing developments in the Quinton and California areas of the City.

Adding a cautionary rider to this decision, the Tramways Committee is concerned lest people should think 'that this proposal should be taken in any way as an indication that tramways generally are becoming obsolete, or that this proposal indicates a policy of abandoning tramways'. When put to the vote, the closure is approved, but not before some Councillors have tried to have the matter 'referred back for further consideration, with a view to the tramway track being relaid for the continuance of running trams'. Also giving rise to concern is the state of the tramway in Bolton Road. This is reported as 'not having met operating expenses from the time of its inception' (1 January 1907), 'and at present there is a net loss of over £500 per annum'. Track relaying will cost £21,000, which will increase the annual loss on the line to over £2,000. Abandonment is recommended, with the substitution of a minimum-level omnibus service, just

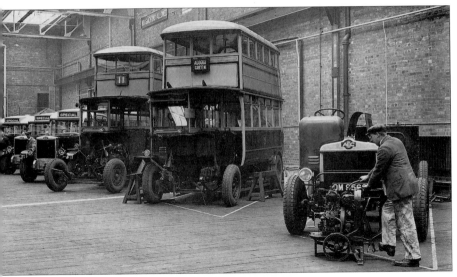

sufficient to cater for passengers in the area. Again, an attempt is made to overturn this decision in Council, which is defeated, as is one to substitute trolleybuses on the line.

5 June — A series of road improvements carried out by the City's Public Works Department enables new and improved omnibus services to commence. The construction of a bridge over a ford in Yardley Wood Road, plus other road widenings, allow a 1,540yd extension to the 13 route along Yardley Wood Road, Glastonbury Road and School Road, as the 13A. Improvements in Hob Moor Road, Yardley, also permit the introduction of a fourth cross-City motor omnibus service, between Yardley and Handsworth Wood, numbered 16 in this direction and 15 in the reverse.

July — With an ever-increasing need for members of the Tramways & Omnibus Engineering Department staff to be mobile, two Morris Cowley Four motor cars are purchased for their use, at £180 each.

August — Postboxes are fitted to the rear of trams and omnibuses. These are emptied by Post Office staff at the City termini. The service is provided until outbreak of war in 1939.

September — Short Bros (Rochester & Bedford) Ltd begins work on the experimental lightweight tramcar body ordered in January. This has been delayed by the non-availability of certain parts.

October — The experimental lightweight tramcar body ordered in January is delivered to Kyotts Lake Road Works and the car is assembled.

Left: Tyburn Road's extensive body shop was the equal of most coachbuilders, and the departments could handle the forming of sheet metal and woodworking, as seen here.
The Electric Railway, Bus & Tram Journal/IAL

Below: Omnibuses went through Tyburn Road Works for a complete overhaul every 50,000 miles in service. They emerged as new, and the attention to detail meant that even the slightest blemish or dent was repaired beforehand.
The Electric Railway, Bus & Tram Journal/IAL

25 October — Alfred Baker, former General Manager of the Corporation Tramways Department, dies aged 69.

November — The experimental lightweight tramcar enters service. It is numbered 842. That same month, 30 six-cylinder AEC Regent double-deck omnibuses are also placed in service. These have pneumatic tyres and enclosed drivers' cabs.

December — After lengthy consideration, an order is placed with the General Electric Co Ltd for the supply of electrical equipment for the experimental lightweight tramcar ordered from Brush in May.

4 December — The opening of the new Tramways & Omnibus Department repair works on the Tyburn Road. Standing on a four-acre site, just 400yd from the Outer Circle route, the works has a ground floor space of 7,187sq yd. It has been designed for the complete overhaul of motor omnibuses, which is to be undertaken after 50,000 miles' service. The works includes the following departments and functions: Sheet Metal; Brake Shoe Grinding; Spring Testing; Smithy; Battery Shop & Charging; Stores; Oil Stores; Boiler House; and Mess Room & Kitchen. The repair facilities at Tennant Street omnibus garage (ex-BMMO) are closed.

31 December — Since its establishment, the Tramways Department has contributed £664,000 to the relief of local rates.

1930: OTHER HISTORIC CONVERSIONS

January — The Joint Traffic Committee becomes a Standing Committee in its own right: the Traffic Control Committee.

Left: Tyburn Road could also perform statutory examinations, such as a tilt test. Here, in April 1931, AEC Regent No 383 has tilted to 37° from the vertical without toppling over.
D. R. Harvey Collection

Top right: With a second tram-to-trolleybus conversion envisaged, attention turned to trying various demonstrators on the Nechells route. Six-wheeled Guy BTX No 18 had a 53 (27/26)-seater body and Rees Turbo equipment. It entered service on 26 February 1930. The advances in trolleybus design since 1922 are very evident here.
Passenger Transport Journal/IAL

Bottom right: No 18, seen here parked up in Nechells, was one of three Guy demonstrators tested, the other two being No 19, an RTX, which was in service between 10 and 17 April 1931, and No 20, a BT, in service from 20 to 27 May 1931. Ultimately, no Guy vehicles were actually purchased, and No 18 was withdrawn from service on 31 July 1931. *Passenger Transport Journal/IAL*

The year also sees two orders of omnibuses, the first being for just 24. Of these, 20 are additional Guy Conquest 25-seater single-deckers, Nos 61-80, the rest being AEC Regents, Nos 209, 338, 339 and 368, with a variety of different bodies, No 209 having an all-metal one by Metropolitan-Cammell. Experience with AEC Regents then leads to a large order for 75 being placed. Thirty-nine, numbered 369-407, have English Electric 48-seat bodies (27/21), and 35, numbered 409-443, the same capacity body by Vulcan; the remaining vehicle is No 408, which has a 47-seat body (26 upper) by English Electric, and a diesel engine, entering service in 1931.

13 February — A siding off the Tyburn Road tramway route is opened to serve to Fort Dunlop.

1 April — The Council instructs the Tramways & Omnibus Committee to report on or introduce a scale of cheaper return tickets for issue to passengers arriving at City termini before 09.00. Replying on 1 July, the Committee notes that the current maximum fare is 7d from the City boundary to the centre. A reduction of fares to a maximum of 4d, which it had set as a goal, is predicted to bring about a loss in revenue of around £21,000, and this is deemed too great to stand at present. As a compromise, it is proposed that 7d and 6d fares be reduced to 5d, causing a loss in revenue of £8,250, which it is hoped might be lessened by increased passenger numbers.

24 April — The Birmingham District Power & Traction Co Ltd sells half its ordinary shares (200,000) in BMMO to the LMS and GWR, and changes its name to the Birmingham & District Investment Trust Ltd, controlled by BET.

4 May — Tramway services along Bolton Road (Route 22) are replaced by omnibuses. These are one-man-operated Guy Conquest single-deckers. The reinstatement of the roadway costs £5,547.

June — Brush delivers its experimental lightweight tramcar body to Kyotts Lake Road Works.

13 July — Albert Street is established as the City terminus. The direction of the one-way tramway movements in Albert Street and Carrs Lane is reversed. This is one of the practical effects of the City's Traffic Control Policy, adopted on 1 March 1927. The reworking of the tramway track and overhead required by this change costs £12,600.

30 July — New omnibus service 23, West Heath-Northfield, is introduced.

August — Tennant Street omnibus garage is reopened for single-deck vehicles only. Also, the new Metropolitan-Cammell all-metal-bodied double-decker omnibus (No 209) is delivered.

11 August — Tramway services along Hagley Road (Route 34) are replaced by omnibuses. Reinstating the roadway after removal of the tramway tracks costs £18,130.

18 August — A new omnibus service, 33, is introduced to serve the large Warren Farm housing estate at Kingstanding from the City.

September — The experimental Brush-bodied lightweight tramcar enters service. It is numbered 843, and runs on Maley & Taunton maximum-traction bogies. The car is the highest

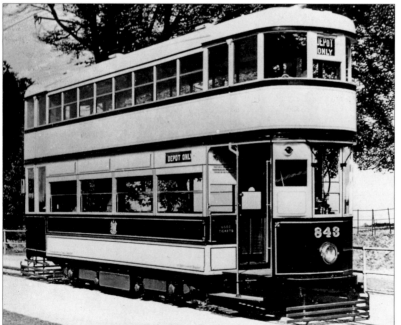

Above: In addition to their regular duties, the Corporation's 'buses also ran special services, such as to the Birmingham Race Course at Castle Bromwich. On a sunny June day in 1930, a quartet of AEC Regents awaits the off in Paradise Street.
G. H. F. Atkins

Left: Birmingham Corporation's final new tram, No 843, had a lightweight body by Brush which incorporated steel, wood and aluminium. Photographed at Rednal in October 1930, the tram was less revolutionary in appearance than No 842, but the body was designed to hide the bogie springing, making the running-gear less conspicuous.
Passenger Transport Journal/IAL

numbered in the Birmingham fleet, and the last new tramcar purchased by the Corporation.

24 September — A new omnibus service, 31, is introduced to link the City with the Gospel Lane housing estate at Fox Hollies.

19 November — New omnibus services begin:

- 18A— Yardley Wood Road-Fitzroy Avenue (Harborne)
- 21— Perry Common-Kingsbury Road (Tyburn House)
- 24— City-Warstock (Yardley)

1931: TRAFFIC SCHEMES

The City's Traffic Control Committee recommends a one-way system for the City centre to relieve traffic congestion. It is proposed that traffic will move anti-clockwise from Victoria Square via New Street, Corporation Street, Bull Street and Colmore Row. This requires Ministry of Transport approval, so, in the short term, High Street is made one-way from Carrs Lane to New Street, and Stephenson Place one-way from New Street. The full scheme is not implemented until 1933.

The year's order for omnibuses is for 70: 10 Morris Dictator single-deckers, numbered 81-90, with 34-seat Metropolitan-Cammell bodies; and 60 AEC Regents, Nos 444-483 having 48-seat bodies by Shorts and Nos 484-503 similar bodies by Metropolitan-Cammell. The original trolleybus fleet is also replaced by 11 Leyland TB2 vehicles, with 48-seater bodies by Shorts, these taking numbers 1-11 in the fleet.

Summer — This is one of the worst on record, with a succession of wet weekends; passenger numbers are adversely affected.

August — The first nine vehicles move into a partially-

Right: The Corporation purchased 10 Morris Dictator single-deckers in 1931 (Nos 81-90), with 34-seater bodies by Metropolitan-Cammel. These were the largest-capacity single-deckers owned by Birmingham to that date. *Modern Transport/IAL*

Left: Another 60 AEC Regents were delivered in 1931 (Nos 444-503), the last 20 of which had 48 (27/21)-seater Metropolitan-Cammell bodies, including No 492 seen here. *IAL*

Below: Vulcan-bodied AEC Regent No 410 appears to be sporting a radiator blind as it works the 6 service to Sandon Road in Colmore Row in August 1931.
G. H. F. Atkins

completed Wellhead Lane (Perry Barr) omnibus garage.

26 December — The Corporation begins its first joint service with a neighbouring authority, when a special omnibus service runs from Carter's Green, West Bromwich, to the St Andrew's football ground.

1932: COMPLETING THE CIRCLES

There are no major vehicle purchases this year, with just five new AEC six-wheeled trolleybuses acquired. Numbered 12-16 in the fleet, they have 58-seat bodies by Brush.

Winter — The weather is unusually fine and mild, producing reduced takings in fares. The Department reckons that a wet morning in winter increases receipts by about £250.

1 February — Omnibus Route 2 is extended to Hamstead from an intermediate terminus in Wellington Road.

16 February — Birchfield Road garage closes on the opening of Perry Barr omnibus garage in Wellhead Lane, which holds 120 vehicles.

2 March — The City Circle, the last of the three Circle omnibus routes, commences. Numbered 19, it runs close-in to the City centre.

1 May — The final stretch of the Washwood Heath tramway route, from Foley Road to the terminus, is replaced by reserved track.

July — A Leyland Titan TD1 48-seat double-deck omnibus is purchased. It has been a demonstration vehicle with the Corporation since 1929, numbered 99, but is fitted with a diesel engine before its purchase.

5 July — The Tramways & Omnibus Committee reports on the Coventry Road tramway. With the exception of the track between Hay Mills Bridge and Holder Road, Hay Mills, the rest (some 6,438yd) is in need of replacement within 12 months at a cost of £27,780. Receipts on the route are also poor: 15.73d per car mile as opposed to the system average of 16.26d. Abandonment of the tramway in favour of

Below: Before the City centre one-way system was introduced on 5 June 1933, 'buses such as AEC Regent No 479 could travel down Corporation Street towards New Street. In August 1931 No 479 was sporting a radiator-mounted destination board, which saved intending passengers from having to look up.
G. H. F. Atkins

Above: Replacements for most of the Nechells trolleybuses finally arrived late in 1931 and entered service during the first week of February 1932. They were 11 Leyland TB2s, with 48 (27/21)-seat bodies by Short Bros. Very 'bus-like in appearance, they had a dummy radiator, as shown by No 1, seen making its way down Corporation Street in May 1932.
G. H. F. Atkins

Left: Like all other Corporation vehicles, the new Leyland TB2s had to undergo a tilt test. AEC Regent No 359 looks on as No 1 approaches 30° at Tyburn Road.
Modern Transport/IAL

Above: A side view of the Leyland TB2 is afforded here by No 11 seen in Old Square. Three of the Railless vehicles (Nos 4, 8 and 12) remained in service after the introduction of the Leylands, until August and September 1932. *W. J. Haynes/IAL*

Below: To complete the replacement of the original Railless trolleybuses, five AEC 663 six-wheeled vehicles were ordered. Numbered 12-16, they entered service in August and September 1932. The full-width cab on these trolleybuses is seen to good effect in this view of No 15. *National Motor Museum*

Top left: Taken on the same occasion, this rear three-quarter view shows No 15's curving lines and the hinged upper rear window emergency exit, a requirement under the Road Traffic Act, 1930. *National Motor Museum*

Bottom left: AEC 663 trolleybus No 15 entered service on 8 September 1932 and is seen five weeks later, on 14 October 1932, waiting in the rain on a trial run to Gosta Green. *The Electric Railway, Bus & Tram Journal/IAL*

Right: Although inherently stable, car No 340 is seen undergoing a tilt test after No 323 overturned in an accident in May 1932. The remains of No 323 can be seen behind on the left. It's 30° and still OK, so far. *IAL*

trolleybuses is recommended, as this offers the largest profit margin at a time of high petrol costs. This is approved, as is loan sanction to purchase 50 trolleybuses at a cost of £95,000.

29 July — The report of the Conference on Rail & Road Transport is published, containing serious implications for the taxation of motor omnibuses and trolleybuses. Work on the conversion of the Coventry Road tramway is therefore suspended until after the Budget in 1933, when the Government's intentions will be known. Ultimately these are not seen as adversely affecting the conversion scheme, and it is then allowed to proceed.

13 August — 10.00am on this date is the deadline for tenders from prospective purchasers of '50 Brill Double Deck Cars seating 49 passengers' which the Corporation has advertised for sale in *The Electric Railway, Bus and Tram Journal*, amongst others. The cars are said to be 'in working order and are at present in service'. Dover Corporation was one successful tenderer in this sale purchasing two of the tramcars plus two bodies which were mounted on under-

frames from withdrawn vehicles. together, these became nos 19-22 in the Dover fleet.

15 August — The Kingstanding-Washwood Heath omnibus service (21) is extended to Bordesley Green East, via Alum Rock Road and Belcher's Lane.

17 October — A new omnibus service (20) is introduced between Weoley Castle and Selly Oak, via Bristol Road, Witherford Way, Shenley Fields Road, Castle Road and Weoley Castle Road.

1933: DIESEL EXPERIMENTS

The year's omnibus purchases total 64, comprising four Morris Dictator single-deckers, numbered 47-50, with 34-seat Metropolitan-Cammell bodies; 50 Morris Imperial double-deckers, numbered 504-553, the first three with one-off bodies, the rest having 50-seat (28/22) all-metal ones by Metropolitan-Cammell; and 10 Daimler CP6 51-seat (29/22) double-deckers, numbered 554-563, with bodies by the Birmingham Railway Carriage & Wagon Works (BRCW).

Above: Birmingham Corporation purchased an extra four Morris Dictator single-deckers in 1933 (Nos 47-50), again with 34-seater bodies by Metropolitan-Cammell. Three of the vehicles are seen awaiting delivery in June 1933. *Passenger Transport Journal/IAL*

Centre left: The bulk of 1933's 'bus orders were for double-deckers, with 50 Morris Imperials and 10 Daimler CP6s. One of the latter, No 557, shows the 51 (29/22)-seater body by the Birmingham Railway Carriage & Wagon Works fitted to the batch. They also had preselector gears, which were found to make driving easy in busy streets. *Modern Transport/IAL*

Bottom left: A striking sight on Birmingham's streets in 1933 was No 93, an AEC Q demonstrator, fitted with a 60 (31/29)-seater Park Royal body. This entered service on 28 January. The Q type had an underfloor engine behind the front wheels, which made forward cabs and front entrances possible. In January 1934 the vehicle was returned to be fitted with an oil (diesel) engine, and was purchased in October 1935. *AEC Equipment Co/IAL*

Above: Another demonstrator used in 1933 was six-wheeled Leyland TTB trolleybus No 17, which ran in service from 11 March to sometime in July. The vehicle returned, this time as No 68, and ran in service in Birmingham from 9 July 1936 until 1 October 1937. *IAL*

Right: Between 1933 and 1935 Guy Conquest single-decker No 60 was equipped to run on town gas. *Passenger Transport Journal/IAL*

THIS BUS IS RUNNING ON TOWN'S GAS

With the forthcoming conversion of the Coventry Road tramway to trolleybus operation, new vehicles are needed. An order is placed for 50 Leyland TTBD2 chassis, with 58-seat all-metal bodies by Metropolitan-Cammell. On delivery they are numbered 17-66 in the fleet. Combined with that for the bodies of the Morris Imperials mentioned above, this is the largest single order for all-metal omnibus bodies placed to date in the UK.

2 January — The Kingstanding-Quinton omnibus services 33 and 34 are extended from Ellerton Road/Warren Farm Road junction to Sidcup Road/Finchley Road junction, via Ellerton Road and Finchley Road.

3 April — The Weoley Castle-Selly Oak omnibus service 20 is extended to Castle Square, via a new route: Weoley Castle Road-Castle Road-Shenley Fields Road-Gibbins Road-Harborne Lane-Chapel Lane-Bristol Road-Weoley Park Road.

17 April — The Kingstanding-Highfield Road omnibus service 29 is extended to Sutton Park, Banner's Gate entrance, via Kingstanding Road, Baker's Lane and Chester Road.

30 April — A summertime Sunday evenings only circular tour omnibus service to the Lickey Hills is inaugurated. This runs from Paradise Street, via Moseley, Yardley Wood and the Outer Circle and Outer Ring routes, and the Bristol Road, returning via Bristol Road, the Outer Circle, the Outer Ring and Hagley Road.

22 May — Kingstanding-Quinton omnibus services 33 and 34 are extended from the junction of Sidcup Road and Finchley Road to King's Road/Finchley Road junction via Finchley Road. Also on this day an omnibus service commences between Snow Hill station and Castle Bromwich aerodrome in connection with the Great Western Railway's new Birmingham-Cardiff-Plymouth air service.

June — Four Morris-Commercial Dictator single-decker petrol buses are placed in service. They have all-metal bodies by Metropolitan-Cammell and seat 34.

4 June — The Livery Street and Colmore Row (Churchyard) tramway termini are transferred to outside Snow Hill station in Colmore Row, save for Routes 24 and 25, which use the top of Snow Hill until 16 September and 7 August respectively.

5 June — A new one-way traffic system is introduced. In preparation for this 28 traffic islands have been constructed and 250 road signs erected; it affects many omnibus routes. A new omnibus route (35) is also introduced: Erdington-City-Alcester Road (Maypole).

4 July — The Tramways & Omnibus Committee reports that it has placed an order for 60 double-deck omnibuses for replacement purposes. It is hoped that they will be in service by the end of September. It also informs the Council that it and the Gas Committee are experimenting with a single-deck omnibus which has been equipped to run on coal gas.

7 August —The Lozells tramway service, via Hamstead Road (Route 25) is withdrawn; those via Wheeler Street are changed to terminate at Villa Cross.

17 September — The City terminus of tramway Route 24 is moved to Livery Street following reconstruction of the Great Hampton Street junction.

Top: Birmingham's second tram-to-trolleybus conversion took place following the closure of the Coventry Road routes to Yardley. These included Route 16, which car No 138 was working on the last day, 6 January 1934, when it was photographed at Hay Mills.
Commercial Postcard/Author's Collection

Above: Fifty six-wheeled Leyland TTBD2 trolleybuses, Nos 17-66, were purchased to work the Coventry Road route. They had 58 (33/25)-seater bodies by Metropolitan-Cammell with full-width cabs and plain fronts. No 19 is pictured on trials just prior to entering service. *Modern Transport/IAL*

Left: Despite having made its largest trolleybus purchase to date, Birmingham Corporation took delivery of another demonstrator early in 1934. A six-wheeled Sunbeam MS2, it had a 59 (31/28)-seater Metropolitan-Cammell body. Entering service on 9 February it ran for just seven weeks, before being withdrawn on 24 March. *IAL*

20 September — Double-deck omnibuses are introduced on the 30 service between Weoley Castle and Selly Oak, and the route is extended from Castle Square via Somerford Road and Gregory Avenue to the Castle Road junction. A new service running in the opposite direction, No 20A, is also introduced.

27 November — Birmingham Corporation puts an experimental Daimler heavy fuel oil-engined (diesel) omnibus into service. The Tramways & Omnibus Department sees the advantages of heavy fuel oil as being that it:

- gives 75% more mileage per gallon than petrol;
- only costs 4.5d per gallon;
- is tax-free;
- has a low fire risk.

13 December — A new omnibus service (14) is introduced between Stechford and Alum Rock, via Flaxley Road, Station Road, Cotterills Lane and Pelham Road.

1934: ANOTHER TROLLEYBUS LINE

After much experimentation, the first of what is to become a standard order for double-deck omnibuses is placed for 70 Daimler COG5 chassis with Gardner 5LW diesel engines, fitted with 48-seat (26/22) bodies built by BRCW or Metropolitan-Cammell. They are delivered in two batches, of 30 (numbers 564-593) and 40 (numbers 594-633).

6 January — Yardley tram services (Routes 13-16, 56, 57) cease. Fifty tramcars are used on the last day of service.

7 January — Yardley tramway services are replaced by trolleybus Routes 56, 57 (Hay Mills from High and Station Streets), 92 and 93 (Yardley from High and Station Streets).

Services are operated by 49 new Leyland six-wheelers, with 58-seat Metropolitan-Cammell bodies. The final bill for these comes to £90,245 6s 3d. With the abandonment of the Coventry Road tramway, the tracks in Station Street, Dudley Street and Pershore Street are only used by tramcars on the Stratford Road route. As a result, the City terminus of tram Route 18 (Hall Green) is transferred to Hill Street from Station Street; ditto Routes 19, 20 and 21, all of which are short workings of the 18. Coventry Road depot becomes joint tramcar/trolleybus on the same day.

21 February — The 23 omnibus service, Northfield-West Heath, is extended from the junction of Redhill Road/Redditch Road, via Redhill Road-Lilley Lane-Alvechurch Road-West Heath Road-Church Hill-Woodland Road. A new service, 23A, is also introduced, which runs in the opposite direction, and a 23B, which works the 23's former West Heath-Norrington Road run.

11 April — The 14 omnibus service is extended to serve the Glebe Farm housing estate in between Stechford and Lea Hall.

4 May — The first of a batch of 30 Daimler COG5 double-decker omnibuses enters service. The order followed extensive trials of vehicles supplied by AEC, Crossley, Daimler, Dennis, Guy, Leyland, Morris Commercial, Tilling-Stevens and Vulcan, conducted between 1930 and 1933. The Daimler chassis will form the basis of 796 double-decker and 35 single-decker omnibuses purchased up to 1939. The bodies are supplied by Metropolitan-Cammell, which has a large works at Washwood Heath.

16 December — A new omnibus service (25) is introduced: Hall Green-Bradford Street-Hill Street-Hockley-Kingstanding, replacing service 29.

Left: On 19 January 1935, 24 Daimler COG5s, with bodies by the BRCW or Metropolitan-Cammell, were lined up to announce the introduction of these vehicles to the press. *Passenger Transport Journal/IAL*

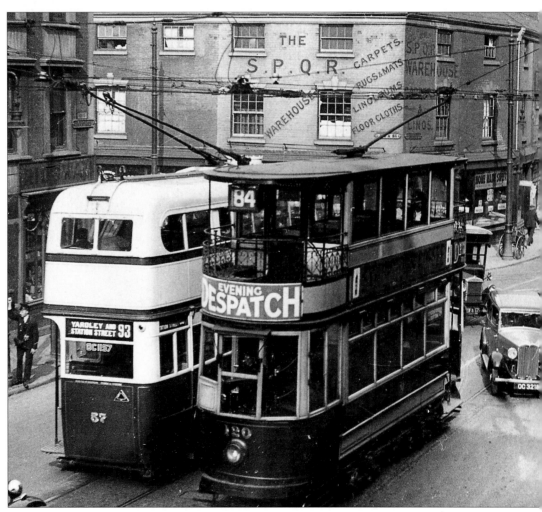

1935: One Bright Tramcar

Another 195 omnibuses are ordered, in three batches. The first is for 60 Daimler COG5 chassis and 48-seat double-deck bodies, numbered 634-693, all but 11 of which are built by the Birmingham Railway Carriage & Wagon Co. Next are 35 Daimler COG5/40 chassis fitted with 34-seat single-deck bodies by Metropolitan-Cammell or Strachans, numbered 42-76. Finally another 100 Daimler COG5 double-deckers are ordered, numbered 694-793, mostly with 48-seat bodies by the Birmingham Railway Carriage & Wagon Co or Metropolitan-Cammell.

2 January — Selly Oak depot accepts omnibuses again. A new omnibus service is introduced between Weoley Castle Estate and Suffolk Street, via California-Harborne-Five Ways-Holloway Head, created by altering the route of service 20.

February — The Traffic Control Committee is reconstituted to include four independent members elected by the Chairman. This move is to cut down delays and bias

BIRMINGHAM CORPORATION TRAMWAY & OMNIBUS DEPT.

Transport Facilities 1935

COUNCIL HOUSE, BIRMINGHAM.

A. C. BAKER GENERAL MANAGER.

Left: Although trolleybuses replaced trams on the Coventry Road, they still shared the streets through Digbeth and Deritend. At the junction with Rea Street, looking towards the City, car No 120 is passed by trolleybus No 57, whilst Nos 18 and 17 chase from behind. This shot was taken on the same occasion as the one on the cover of this book. *Birmingham Post & Mail*

Top right: Now the operator of three different kinds of public transport vehicle, Birmingham Corporation celebrated the fact with this cover art on its 1935 timetable and map. Only trolleybus No 19 is identified, although the tram is clearly one between Nos 762-841, and the 'bus is a Daimler COG5. *Author's Collection*

Right: The Corporation did a fair trade in disposing of its withdrawn 'buses, but some were retained and converted into service vehicles. One such was AEC 504 No 147 of 1925, which was converted into service vehicle No 9 upon withdrawal in 1935. *IAL*

OM 9561

caused by the 'conflicting interests' of the various Council committees represented.

Spring — A site for the erection of a motor omnibus garage is purchased in Liverpool Street. This will accommodate 150 omnibuses, and will be constructed from structural steelwork.

6-11 May — An illuminated tramcar tours the City to celebrate the Silver Jubilee of King George V and Queen Mary. Car No 63 is bedecked with lights, swags, and other decorations, bearing the illuminated message:

GOD BLESS
OUR
KING AND QUEEN
SILVER JUBILEE
1910 – 1935

with the message being in white bulbs, the dates in red. At 9.30pm the car sets out for a different part of the City, working round it anti-clockwise:

Above: Daimler COG5 chassis rapidly became the hoice for Birmingham Corporation, and in 1935 it took delivery of 35 single-deck versions (Nos 42-76). The last 15 of the batch had 34-seater bodies by Strachan, including No 75 seen here just before entering service.
Modern Transport/IAL

Left: The largest 'bus order yet made by the Corporation was placed in 1935, for 100 Daimler COG5 double-deckers. Work on the bodies was split 50/50 between Metropolitan-Cammell-Weymann and BRCW, that for No 726 being the handiwork of the former.
The Electric Railway, Bus & Tram Journal/IAL

Above: Between 6 and 11 May 1935 an illuminated tramcar toured the City to celebrate the Silver Jubilee of King George V and Queen Mary. Car No 63 was bedecked in lights, swags and other decorations, and carried the illuminated message: 'GOD BLESS OUR KING AND QUEEN — SILVER JUBILEE 1910-1935'. *IAL*

- 6 May (southeast) — Kyotts Lake Road-Navigation Street-Hall Green-Warwick Road-Kyotts Lake Road;
- 7 May (east) — Washwood Heath-Alum Rock-Dale End-Stechford via Fazeley Street-Bordesley Station via Cattell Road-Kyotts Lake Road;
- 8 May (northeast) — Miller Street-Pype Hayes-Erdington-Short Heath-Dale End-Kyotts Lake Road;
- 9 May (north and northwest) — Martineau Street-Perry Barr-Witton via Six Ways-Handsworth-Oxhill Road-Colmore Row-Dale End-Kyotts Lake Road;
- 10 May (west) — Navigation Street-Ladywood-Grove Lane, Dudley Road-Edmund Street-Lodge Road-Edmund Street-Icknield Port Road-Ladywood Terminus-Navigation Street-Kyotts Lake Road;
- 11 May (southwest and south) — Chapel Lane-Northfield-Cotteridge via Pebble Mill Road and Pershore Road-Navigation Street-King's Heath via Balsall Heath-Moseley Road/Bradford Street junction-Kyotts Lake Road.

These journeys include a number of unusual workings, especially that from Northfield to Cotteridge via Pebble Mill Road and the Pershore Road on 11 May.

2 July — The Tramways & Omnibus Committee reports to the Council that, since 3 July 1934, it has placed orders for 200 double-deck and 35 single-deck omnibuses, of which 215 have been delivered and placed in service. These have allowed the withdrawal of older vehicles, and as of this date only 53 of the 'old type' omnibuses remain in service. Regarding a decrease

in the transport undertaking's net profit of £6,418 in the year to 31 March 1935, it is remarked that this 'is due in a large measure to the development of the housing estates on the outskirts of the City, which has necessitated additional services being provided at peak load times which operate at an uneconomic fare'.

1 October — New omnibus service 26 commences: King's Heath-Bournbrook, via Vicarage Road-Avenue Road-Dads Lane-Dogpool Lane-St Stephen's Road-Warwards Lane-Raddlebarn Road-Dawlish Road; also a new omnibus service 27: King's Heath-Hay Green, via Vicarage Road-Avenue Road-Dads Lane-Pineapple Road-Cartland Road-Pershore Road-Hazelwell Street-Bournville Lane-Linden Road-Woodbrooke Road-Bournville Lane-Hay Green Lane-Woodlands Park Road. From this day too, service 22 (Station Street-Bolton Road) is connected to a new service 28: Kingstanding-Bordesley Green East, via Oldknow Road-St Benedicts Road-Yardley Green Road-Belcher's Lane.

22 October — Birchfield Road garage reopens.

6. 1936-1939: The All-Conquering Omnibus

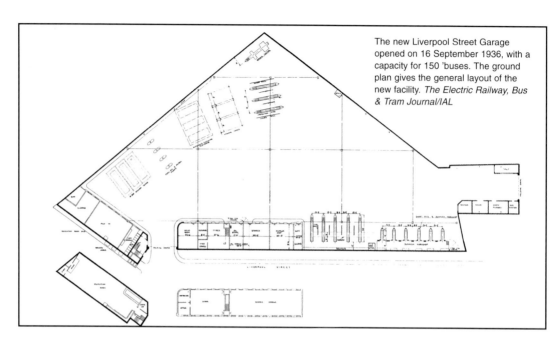

The new Liverpool Street Garage opened on 16 September 1936, with a capacity for 150 'buses. The ground plan gives the general layout of the new facility. *The Electric Railway, Bus & Tram Journal/IAL*

On entering the new Liverpool Street Garage, 'buses proceeded to the fuel oil pumps, where Daimler COG5 No 846 is parked, and where Nos 854 and 819 have just been. *The Electric Railway, Bus & Tram Journal/IAL*

By the mid-1930s, despite an expertly-maintained tramway system, an increasing majority of Birmingham's road public transport needs were being met by diesel omnibuses. Between 1936 and 1939 the City would order 667 of these vehicles, 24 trolleybuses, and no tramcars. In the first of these years, the motor omnibus would exceed the tramcar as top revenue-earner for the first time; the following year it would come out top on all counts. Nine new omnibus services would be introduced and others extended and modified, whilst two major sets of tramway routes, the Stratford and Dudley Road groups, closed. In the City, the Council tightened its control of traffic flows, introducing two one-way systems, with portents of more to come — changes which omnibuses could take in their stride, but against which track-bound tramcars stood no chance. More tramway closures were planned for 1940, but in September 1939, a former Birmingham Lord Mayor shattered the peace of a late summer Sunday morning with an historic radio broadcast.

1936: HISTORIC FIGURES

The cost of removing old tramlines is agreed at 7s 6d per square yard, including making good the road surface. This is to be paid by the Tramways & Omnibus Committee to the Public Works Committee. The year's omnibus order totals 110, and includes 10 Daimler COG5/40 chassis fitted with 34-seat single-deck bodies by Metropolitan-Cammell, numbered 32-41. There are also another 100 Daimler COG5 double-deckers, numbered 794-893, with 48-seat bodies by BRCW or Metropolitan-Cammell.

1 January — New omnibus service 29 commences: Baldwins Lane (Hall Green)-Kingstanding (King's Road) via Baldwins Lane-Scribers Lane-Kedleston Road-Robin Hood Lane-Sarehole Road-Colebank Road-Wake Green Road-Springfield Road, then as Route 29. The Gospel Lane (Fox Hollies) service 31 is also extended from this date, via Tavistock Road-Broomhall Crescent-Gospel Lane-Redstone Farm Road-Westhay Road-Arkley Road-Sleaford Road-Lakey Lane-Fox Hollies Road-School Road-Stratford Road to the City, becoming new service No 31A. Run in the opposite direction, from the City, is new service 32, and collectively these are known as the Gospel Lane Loop.

31 March — The financial year 1935/6 proves an historic one for the Corporation transport undertaking. For the first time in its history, the gross revenue from the omnibus service (£1,184,870) exceeds that from the tramways (£1,107,949), although the latter still carries 23,760,960 more passengers, and has 143 more vehicles. In the past year £171,905 has been spent on 100 new double-deck omnibuses, and £62,982 on 45 single-deckers.

5 July — The Yardley trolleybus service is extended to Sheldon, at a cost of £8,250. Two new routes are introduced, 94 and 95, from High Street and Station Street.

7 July — The Tramways & Omnibus Committee reports to the Council on the condition of the tramway fleet. It has currently in operation 254 tramcars of an obsolete design, which have been in service since 1907. It is felt that 'it would be in the best interests of the travelling public to abandon certain tramways as the tracks fall in for renewal and to substitute some other form of vehicle and so gradually dispose of these old tramcars'.

Below: From the fuel oil pumps 'buses entering Liverpool Street Garage went for a wash-down, after which they were manoeuvred to the inspection pits, seen below, or took up position for their next turn of duty. *The Electric Railway, Bus & Tram Journal/IAL*

To illustrate this point, the cases of the Warwick Road tramway, and the Stratford Road one from Kyotts Lake Road to St John's Road, are highlighted. These are reported to be in need of relaying in the next 12 months, at a cost of £59,000. To do so would then require the remaining portion of the track on the routes, plus Stoney Lane, to be relaid, at an additional £61,000. Receipts from these tramways to 31 March are 14.26d per car mile, below the City average of 15.799d. Currently, seven omnibus services use the Stratford Road, requiring 103 vehicles, and it is felt that 'it will be possible by an adjustment of these services to meet the requirements of the travelling public by the addition of fewer vehicles than the number of tramcars displaced'. Accordingly, the abandonment of the Warwick Road and Stratford Road tramways is recommended.

The question of the 4d Workmen's fare, first raised in 1930, has not gone away. Last reported on in October 1935, the Council ordered the Tramways & Omnibus Committee to report back to it at the end of the financial year 1935/6. The Committee has done its homework. After citing all the expenditure to which it is committed (mainly tramway conversions, new omnibuses, and a drivers' and conductors' pay rise of 2s 6d due in July), it replies that this is not practicable. To underscore this, figures are provided, comparing Birmingham's 5d Workmen's return fare stages with those in Bradford, Leeds, Liverpool, London, Manchester, Nottingham, Sheffield, Edinburgh and Glasgow. These show that 'no town has such cheap fares as Birmingham'.

16 August — The City's one-way traffic system is extended to include Hill Street, Paradise Street and Edmund Street. This provides three gyratory traffic systems which interlock like cogwheels. It is noted that traffic could continue to flow around these indefinitely, but for the need to allow pedestrians to cross!

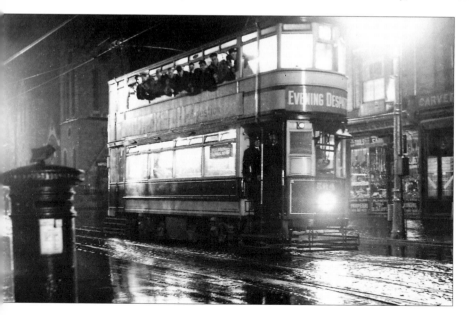

16 September — Birchfield Road garage closes on the opening of Liverpool Street, a purpose-built omnibus garage which has capacity for 150 vehicles. Semi-(light) overhauls are still carried out at Birchfield Road for four months.

21 September — New omnibus route 36 begins: Station Street-Stratford Road-Formans Road-Berkeley Road East-Stechford.

11 December — A one-way traffic scheme is introduced at Five Ways, Edgbaston, necessitated by the speeding up of traffic flows through the City following the one-way system introduced there on 16 August.

1937: OMNIBUS SUPRA OMNES

The year's omnibus order, for no fewer than 245 vehicles, plus 12 trolleybuses, is a record. The latter are Leyland TB5s, with 53-seat bodies by Metropolitan-Cammell; numbered 67-78, they are delivered in the autumn. Omnibuses are ordered in four batches. First are 70 Daimler COG5 double-deckers, numbered 894-963, with 54-seat bodies (30/24) by Metropolitan-Cammell. Next are five Leyland Titans with TD4c chassis and Leyland's own 52-seat body (28/24); numbered 964-968, these use a 'torque converter' gearless transmission, which, it is hoped, will prove easier for ex-tramcar drivers to master. Ordered at the same time are a further 31 Daimler COG5 double-deckers, numbered 969-999, with 54-seat bodies (30/24) by Metropolitan-Cammell, followed by another 34 of the same, to be numbered 1000-1033. Finally come five AEC Regents, with 54-seat Metropolitan-Cammell bodies, numbered 1034-1038, and another 100 Daimler COG5s, again with 54-seat Metro-Cammell bodies, numbered 1039-1138.

5 January — The Hall Green and intermediate Stratford Road tramway Routes 4, 17-21, 44, 82, 83, 89 and 91, including services to Tyseley, Acocks Green and Stoney Lane, are converted to omnibus operation. Some routes retain their numbers, while others are renumbered (17 to 37, 18 to 46, 82 to 38), and new Route 47 is introduced: Station Street-Hall Green.

6 January — Highgate Road depot is closed for conversion to an omnibus garage, at a cost of £6,500; it reopens in June.

Above: The scene in Highgate Road depot at 2.00am on 6 January 1937, following the closure of the Stratford Road tramway routes. Route indicators had been turned to show the numbers of routes formerly worked from the depot, including the 22, closed in 1930. *W. A. Camwell/National Tramway Museum*

Below: Page 69 of the *Rules & Regulations* issued by the Tramways & Omnibus Department in May 1937 contained this warning to Motormen on the identification of low-bridge cars for use on certain routes. *Author's Collection*

69

Low Bridge Cars.

The following "Low Bridge Car" Regulations must always be strictly observed :—

> **LOW BRIDGE CAR.**
> **SELLY OAK. ASTON.**
> **DUDLEY PORT.**

Cars bearing the above plate attached to the Signal Light Rails **will pass under the Low Bridges at Selly Oak, Aston Station and Dudley Port.**

Cars bearing this plate attached to the stair risers **will pass under Selly Oak Bridge** (Rednal Route), but **will not go under the Bridges at Aston Station and Dudley Port.**

Cars bearing this plate attached to the stair risers **will pass under Aston Station and Selly Oak Bridges, but will not go under the Bridge at Dudley Port.**

Under no circumstances are cars to be driven under the Selly Oak, Aston Station or Dudley Port Bridges unless bearing the necessary Low Bridge Car Plate.

13 January — New omnibus service 3A is introduced: City-Harborne-Ridgacre Road.

26 January — Birchfield Road garage closes.

31 March — End-of-year figures show the omnibus service to be supreme in all statistics: miles run, passengers carried, number of vehicles and gross revenue. Allied to this is the expenditure during the year of £317,372 on 171 new double-deck omnibuses.

6 July — In its report to the Council the Tramways & Omnibus Committee notes work in hand to extend Tyburn Road repair works, and that it has recently purchased a site in Yardley Wood for the erection of a motor omnibus garage to accommodate 150 vehicles. This is estimated to cost £110,000. As a sign of difficulties to come, it is also reported that owing to a dwindling number of suppliers, the Department has had to place certain contracts for tramway items, in contradiction of Council Standing Orders requiring competing tenders to be obtained. These are for worm wheels and shafts, tram seats, and steel tramway tyres.

27 October — New omnibus service 16A begins: Yardley (Barrows Lane)-City-Beauchamp Avenue (Great Barr).

9 November — The Department's name is changed, from Birmingham Corporation Tramways & Omnibus Department, to Birmingham City Transport.

1938: END OF THE LINES

A single batch of 99 Daimler COG5s, numbered 102-200, with 54-seat bodies by the BRCW or Metropolitan-Cammell,

BRIDGES

SPECIAL INSTRUCTION TO 'BUS DRIVERS

Under no circumstances is a double-decked omnibus to be driven under any bridge off a recognised double-decked 'bus route until the Driver has definitely satisfied himself that it is high enough for the 'bus to pass under with safety.

Low Bridges on Recognised Double Decked 'Bus Routes

Robin Hood Lane (Kingstanding—Baldwin's Lane Service No. 29A).

Icknield Street (Inner Circle Service No. 8).

Lincoln Road (Carrs Lane—Lincoln Road North Service No. 44A).

'Buses which will not pass under the above low bridges are equipped with a pale yellow steering wheel and a low-bridge warning plate in the Driver's cabin worded: **"This 'bus must not run under Robin Hood Lane, Icknield Street or Lincoln Road Bridges."**

Drivers are instructed that under no circumstances must any attempt be made to pass under the above bridges with one of these 'buses.

Note.—All omnibuses of the Department will safely pass under any bridges over a tramway route in the City of Birmingham. Great care is necessary when proceeding under arched bridges.

This slip to be gummed into the Rule Book between pages 38 and 39.

Top left: A similar warning was issued to the drivers of double-deck omnibuses in the same rule book. *Author's Collection*

Bottom left: 1937's order for Daimler COG5s was for a mere 70, of which No 914 was a part. The 54 (30/24)-seater body was by Metropolitan-Cammell, but most interest seems to be focused upon the sale of some flowers, in which one of the Tramways & Omnibus Department's staff appears to be engaged. *IAL*

Top right: With former tramway motormen and conductors to be trained as 'bus drivers, the Transport Department was always on the look-out for anything which might make this process easier. One hope was the Leyland TD4c, which featured a 'Gearless' transmission. Five such vehicles were delivered in April 1937, Nos 964-968, the last of which is seen here. *IAL*

Below: One feature of the Leyland 'gearless' 'buses was an escape window on the nearside of the driver's cab which was opened by a quick-release catch, as seen demonstrated here. *Passenger Transport Journal/IAL*

Centre right: Another illuminated car was produced for the Coronation of King George VI and Queen Elizabeth in May 1937. Again based on car No 63, this was drastically cut-down to feature a crown more prominently. *Passenger Transport Journal/IAL*

Bottom right: The first 'bus of the second batch of vehicles delivered in 1937 was given the fleet number 1000, and later in the year another order of 100 Daimler COG5s was delivered, including Metropolitan-Cammell 54 (30/24)-seat bodied No 1053, seen here. *The Electric Railway, Bus & Tram Journal/IAL*

Above: Corporation 'buses did good business on private charters, as demonstrated by this party at Halford Works, Smethwick, on 3 July 1937, with Morris Imperial No 551 of 1933. *H. F. Wheeler/D. R. Harvey Collection*

Below: Amidst calls for dental hygiene and for express travel, people are acting as though they are in a film as Daimler COG5 No 1023 crosses the junction between Navigation Street and Hill Street in August 1937. On the left, a young woman is agitated as a Midland Red 'bus swings round into Hill Street. *G. H. F. Atkins*

Right: The ticketing and fare arrangements for services to West Bromwich remained complicated until 1967. To aid comprehension this is what conductors were told in the *Fare Guide* for 1937. *Author's Collection*

Below: Victoria Square was a popular loading place for Corporation 'buses until its destruction in the late 1960s. With the Council House as backdrop, Daimler COG5 No 664 of 1935 pulls away after depositing two passengers. *Modern Transport/IAL*

WEST BROMWICH FARES.

No. 74—Dudley (via West Bromwich).

Between	Ord.	Child	W'kmen's S'gle	W'kmen's Ret.
Boundary and Hope Street ...	1d.	½d.	—	—
Hope Street and Carters Green	1d.	½d.	—	—
Carters Green and Charles St.	1d.	½d.	—	—
Swan Lane and Great Bridge	1d.	½d.	—	—
Great Bridge and Sedgley Rd.	1d.	½d.	—	—
Dudley Port Stn. and Dudley Stn.	1d.	½d.	—	—
Boundary and Spon Lane ...	1½d.	1d.	1d.	2d.
Boundary and Carters Green	2d.	1d.	—	3d.
Hope St. and Charles St. ...	2d.	1d.	—	3d.
Carters Green and Gt. Bridge	2d.	1d.	—	2d.
Swan Lane and Sedgley Road	2d.	1d.	—	—
Great Bridge and Dudley Stn.	2d.	1d.	—	3d.
Boundary and Charles Street	3d.	1½d.	—	4d.
Hope Street and Great Bridge	3d.	1½d.	—	—
Carters Green and Sedgley Rd.	3d.	1½d.	—	3d.
Swan Lane and Dudley Stn. ...	3d.	1½d.	—	4d.
Boundary and Great Bridge...	4d.	2d.	—	5d.
Hope Street and Sedgley Road	4d.	2d.	—	—
Carters Green and Dudley Stn.	4d.	2d.	—	5d
Boundary and Sedgley Road	5d.	2½d.	—	6d.
Hope Street and Dudley Stn.	5d.	2½d.	—	6d.
Boundary and Dudley Station	6d.	3d.	—	7d.
Beeches Rd. and Carters Green	—	—	1d.	2d.
Dartmouth St. and Charles St.	—	—	1d.	—
Charles St. and Dudley Port Station	—	—	1d.	—
Beeches Rd. and Great Bridge	—	—	—	4d.
Beeches Rd. and Sedgley Rd.	—	—	—	5d.

14

WEST BROMWICH FARES.

No. 75—Wednesbury.

Between	Ord.	Child	W'kmen's S'gle	W'kmen's Ret.
Boundary and Hope Street ...	1d.	½d.	—	—
Hope St. and Carters Green ...	1d.	½d.	—	—
Carters Green and Hawkes Lane	1d.	½d.	—	—
Hawkes Lane and White Horse	1d.	½d.	—	—.
Boundary and Spon Lane ...	1½d.	1d.	1d.	2d.
Boundary and Carters Green	2d.	1d.	—	3d.
Hope Street and Hawkes Lane	2d.	1d.	—	3d.
Carters Green and White Horse	2d.	1d.	—	3d.
Boundary and Hawkes Lane	3d.	1½d.	—	4d.
Hope Street and White Horse	3d.	1½d.	—	4d.
Boundary and White Horse ...	4d.	2d.	—	5d.
Beeches Rd. and Carters Green	—	—	1d.	2d.
Dartmouth St. and Hawkes Lane	—	—	1d.	—
Swan Lane and White Horse	—	—	1d.	—

15

enters service this year. These take the numbers of now-withdrawn vehicles supplied in the 1920s.

31 March — The Transport Department's end-of-year figures show that it has spent £323,976 on the 175 new motor omnibuses delivered during the year.

21 September — Following the completion of new roads, omnibus service 14, Old Square-Glebe Village, is extended via Kitts Green Road to the junction at Lea Village.

25 September — Tramway lines are diverted from High Street, Erdington, to Sutton New Road; these are the last new tramlines laid in the City. The High Street tracks are abandoned.

9 November — Yardley Wood purpose-built omnibus garage opens in Yardley Wood Road. It has capacity for 150 vehicles.

23 November — Omnibus service 15B is introduced: City-Yardley-Garretts Green Lane.

1939: NO MORE AGREEMENT

Over 200 new omnibuses enter service during the year, being the majority of 214 ordered in three batches. The first is for 85 Leyland Titan TD6c chassis, fitted with 52-seat (28/24) Metropolitan-Cammell bodies, numbered 211-295. Next come 96 Daimler COG5 double-deckers, numbered 1140-1235, with 54-seat bodies by Metropolitan-Cammell, followed by another 34 of the same, numbered 1236-1269, four with one-off bodies and 30 bodied by BRCW. The trolleybus fleet is also set to be strengthened, with an order

placed for 12 Leyland TB7s, with 54-seat bodies by Metropolitan-Cammell, which are delivered early in 1940 as Nos 79-90.

1 January — The agreement with the Birmingham & District Investment Trust, under which the Corporation now operated the Dudley Road group of tramways, expires. Dudley Corporation already owns the track in its borough, and Smethwick, Oldbury, Rowley Regis and Tipton Corporations have signalled their intention to purchase the tramways in their respective areas, with a view to their abandonment and replacement with omnibus services provided jointly by Birmingham Corporation and BMMO. This move requires Parliamentary sanction, and in the interim it is agreed that the present tramway service will continue until 1 January 1940, on the same terms as the existing agreement. Unusually, for a tramway considered for abandonment, the services are profitable, but their abandonment will cause problems for the Ladywood and Lodge Road tramways, served by Rosebery Street depot. To maintain these services after the abandonment of the Dudley Road group of lines will require the maintenance of 2,794yd of track for depot access and entry into the City for the Lodge Road line. Operation of this is seen as being uneconomic; closure it also affords an opportunity to get rid of a number of tramcars, which are small and of an obsolete design, the tight curves on the route being seen as preventing the use of larger tramcars of more modern design. These conversions are costed at £183,000, comprising £168,000 for 80 new

The route to Bearwood had exactly one month left to operate when No 190 was photographed there on 30 August 1938. Until 1930 the Corporation's Hagley Road route had terminated just around the corner by the King's Head pub. *W. A. Camwell/National Tramway Museum*

omnibuses, £13,500 for the conversion of Rosebery Street depot, and £1,500 for garage machinery and plant.

1 January — The opening of the Queen Elizabeth Hospital is met by an extension of the Ivy Bush-Hamstead omnibus service 2 to Dawlish Road, via Richmond Hill and the hospital, creating new service 2B.

10 January — The Transport Committee reports that the Public Works Committee has advised it of a proposal to carry out road improvements in Digbeth, High Street, Deritend and High Street, Bordesley, requiring the removal of the tram tracks from their present position. As a result, the last date upon which tramcars could operate on the existing track would be 31 March 1940. Only the Stechford service, 84, uses these, and receipts from it, at 14.06d per car mile, are lower than the City average: 15.76d. The reconstruction would be along a central reservation between Rea and Adderley Streets, at a cost of £10,500. Other portions of the track would also need to be reconstructed in the near future, at a cost of £29,500, and reconstruction of the remainder of the line, excepting 1,530yd of sleeper track between Belcher's Lane and Stechford, would bring the total to £76,000.

Right: Many additional 'buses were purchased pending the conversion of the tramway routes worked from Hockley depot on 2 April 1939. These included 85 Leyland TD6cs, of which No 290 was one. Its body was by Metropolitan-Cammell and seated 52 (28/24). *Modern Transport/IAL*

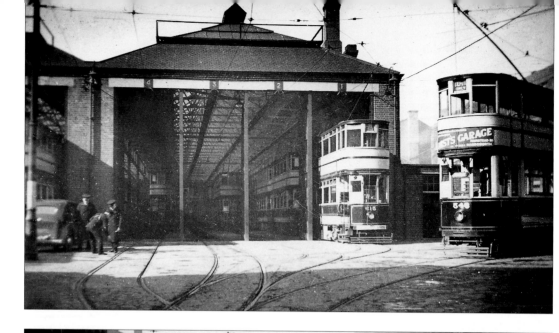

Top left: One month before its closure as a tram depot, things seem pretty much as usual at Hockley on 1 March 1939. The depot had been opened in 1888 for the Handsworth cable trams.
R. T. Coxon/National Tramway Museum

Centre left: Also closed on 1 April 1939 were tramway routes using Wheeler Street, including the 24 to Lozells. Car No 594 was photographed working the route on 13 March 1939.
H. B. Priestley/National Tramway Museum

Bottom left: On 31 March 1939, the day before closure, car No 535 turns on Route 26 from Grove Lane into Soho Road on its return to Colmore Row.
H. P. Priestley/National Tramway Museum

Top right: Departing the City terminus of the 74 route to Dudley, car No 516 rounds the curve into Colmore Row from Livery Street on 31 March 1939.
H. B. Priestley/National Tramway Museum

Centre right: The closure of Hockley depot and the routes it served permitted the withdrawal of many older tramcars. Most of these were sold for scrap, and Nos 168 and 101 were broken up at West Smethwick depot later in 1939. Their remains are seen above.
Author's Collection

Bottom right: Enjoying its last spring, the Edmund Street-Oldbury-Dudley Route 87 was being worked by car No 95 on 12 April 1939.
H. B. Priestley/National Tramway Museum

Abandonment of the tramway is therefore recommended on 31 March 1940, to be replaced by omnibuses. Trolleybuses are not recommended, owing to their inflexibility should the impending war materialise. Fifty new omnibuses will be required, at a cost of £105,000; these can be accommodated in Liverpool Street garage.

8 February — Omnibus service 13B is introduced: City-Showell Green Lane-Billesley Lane; this runs until 10 September.

1 April — Tramway services to Handsworth, Oxhill Road and Wheeler Street, and the Dudley and Wednesbury Routes 23, 24, 26, 28, 73, 74, 75, 76 and 77, are discontinued and converted to omnibus operation, which begins on 2 April. Some routes are renumbered (24 to 69, 26 to 70, 28 to 71, 23 to 72), and new services are introduced: 78, Colmore Row-Dudley Port, via West Bromwich; and 79, Colmore Row-Hill Top, via West Bromwich; services 71-79 being run jointly with West Bromwich Corporation. The Dudley and Wednesbury routes are operated jointly by Birmingham and West Bromwich Corporations, and a tramway practice, whereby passengers have to purchase new tickets at the boundary, is perpetuated when the omnibuses take over, only ceasing on 27 August 1967!

2 April — Albion depot closes entirely, and Hockley depot is extended and converted for omnibuses, the work being completed by October at a cost of £25,932. Omnibus Route 44A is also introduced: Albert Street-Lincoln Road North (Acocks Green).

6 June — The Traffic Control Committee becomes the Traffic Advisory Committee, as members feel it is both under-resourced and duplicating the work of other Committees. Hereafter its role becomes one of an arbitrator in disputes between other Standing Committees of the Council.

4 July — In its report to the Council the Transport Committee notes that it has spent £168,512 on the purchase of 85 new omnibuses for the West Bromwich routes.

24 July — The Perry Common omnibus service, No 5, is extended to Court Lane via Witton Lodge Road, and renumbered 5A in this direction only.

3 September — At 11.00am, a Birmingham man, The Prime Minister, Neville Chamberlain, Lord Mayor of the City during the last war, in 1915, declares war on Germany.

Left: Slated for closure, but reprieved by the war, was the Lodge Road route. It was being worked by car No 61 on 27 July 1939. The Railway pub, on the right, is now abandoned and forlorn. *H. B. Priestley/National Tramway Museum*

Bottom left: Interlaced track was uncommon on the Birmingham tramway system. A rare example was in Oldbury Road where car No 185 working Route 37 is approaching Roebuck Lane on 23 August 1939, just five weeks before closure. *W. A. Camwell/National Tramway Museum*

Above: Passing the entrance to Tividale depot is car No 84 as it works the 87 route back to Birmingham from Dudley via Oldbury. The closure of this route on 30 September 1939 ended tramway operation in the Black Country. *H. B. Priestley/National Tramway Museum*

Below: At Dudley, Corporation car No 88 waits to depart for Birmingham on Route 87, whilst a Midland Red 'bus for Stourbridge is parked up outside Dudley garage. The tram would be withdrawn in May 1939, just four months before the route closed in the early weeks of the war. *A. D. Packer/National Tramway Museum*

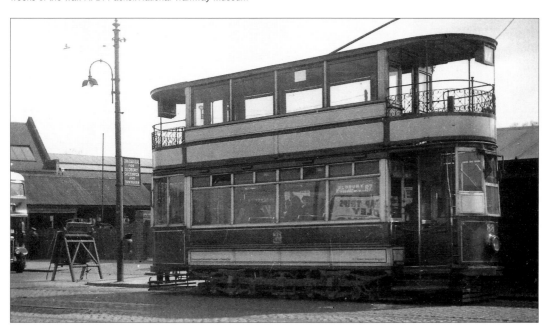

Appendix 1. Birmingham Transport Timetables, 1905

These timetables have been derived from information presented in *Allday's Dictionary of Birmingham*, for which no date of publication is given. The above date has been estimated from the services which are (and are not) listed, plus other dates and information presented in the volume, which place it between March 1905 and March 1906. Birmingham was a veritable feast of public transport in 1905, with four different forms of tramway traction — cable, electric, horse and steam — and both horse and motor buses, all plying their trade along the City's streets.

Birmingham Corporation (*Electric tramcar services*)

Witton-Steelhouse Lane

Weekdays	8.00am, then frequently until 11.04pm
Sundays	10.08am, then every 40min until 1.28pm, then every 20min until 10.38pm

Steelhouse Lane-Aston Cross

Weekdays	5.26am, then frequently until 11.26pm
Sundays	10.26am, then frequently until 11.06pm

Aston Cross-Steelhouse Lane

Weekdays	5.16am, then frequently until 11.16pm
Sundays	10.16am, then frequently until 10.56pm

Aston Cross-Witton

Weekdays	5.36am, then frequently until 11.36pm
Sundays	10.36am, then frequently until 10.56pm

Gravelly Hill-Aston Cross

Weekdays	5.40am, then frequently until 11.35pm
Sundays	10.08am, then every 4min until 10.52pm

Aston Cross-Gravelly Hill

Weekdays	5.30am, then frequently until 11.35pm
Sundays	9.58am, then every 4min until 10.42pm

Six Ways-Aston Cross

Weekdays	7.00am, then 20min service until 10.40pm
Sundays	2.00pm, then 20min service until 10.20pm

Aston Cross-Six Ways

Weekdays	6.50am, then 20min service until 10.30pm
Sundays	1.50pm, then 20min service until 10.10pm

Six Ways-Aston Station

Weekdays	7.10am, then 20min service until 10.50pm
Sundays	2.10pm, then 20min service until 10.30pm

Aston Station-Six Ways

Weekdays	7.20am, then 20min service until 10.40pm
Sundays	2.20pm, then 20min service until 10.20pm

Birmingham & Midland Tramways

Allday's use of the BMT title to describe the tramway services listed below is a little misleading. They do include the BMT services, but also those operated by the City of Birmingham Tramways Co; both companies being controlled by BET. (*Note: The type of traction is indicated with each timetable*)

Edmund Street-Windmill Lane (ELECTRIC)

Weekdays	5.15am, then every few minutes until 11.45pm
Saturdays	5.15am, then every few minutes until 12.10am
Sundays	9.15am, then every few minutes until 11.20pm

Windmill Lane-Edmund Street

Weekdays	5.00am, then every few minutes until 11.25pm
Saturdays	5.00am, then every few minutes until 11.50pm
Sundays	9.00am, then every few minutes until 11.00pm

Edmund Street-Dudley (ELECTRIC)

Weekdays	5.15am, then every 30min until 10.20pm; 10.40pm and 10.50pm to Spon Lane only
Sundays	9.30am, then frequent service to 10.00pm; 10.10pm to Spon Lane only

Dudley-Edmund Street

Weekdays	5.18am, 6.15, then every 30min until 10.45pm
Saturdays	5.18am, 6.15, then every 30min until 11.15pm
Sundays	10.00am, then every hour until 2.00pm, then every 20min until 9.30pm; 10.20pm and 11.00pm to Spon Lane only

Hill Street-Balsall Heath
(Coach & Horses, Mary Street) (STEAM)

Daily	5.45am, 6.55, then every 10min until 7.25am, then every 4/5min until 11.41pm

Balsall Heath
(Coach & Horses, Mary Street)-Hill Street

Daily	5.27am, 6.35, 6.47, 6.57 and 7.07, then every 4/5min until 11.23pm

Navigation Street-Bournbrook (Chapel Lane) (ELECTRIC)

Weekdays	5.20am, then frequent service until 11.37pm
Sundays	9.57am, then every 5min until 11.07pm

Bournbrook (Chapel Lane)-Navigation Street

Weekdays	4.55am, then frequent service until 11.01pm
Sundays	9.30am, then every 5min until 10.40pm

Colmore Row-Hockley Brook (CABLE)

Weekdays	5.30am, 5.45, then frequent service until 11.50pm
Sundays	9.35am and every 4min until 2.35pm, then every 2min until 10.55pm

Hockley Brook-Colmore Row

Weekdays	5.15am, 5.30, 5.45, 5.48, 5.55, 6.05, 6.15, 6.30, and frequent service until 11.35pm
Sundays	9.22am, then every 4min until 2.36pm, then every 4min until 10.50pm

Hill Street-King's Heath via Balsall Heath (STEAM)

Weekdays	5.45am, 7.30, then every 9min until 11.41pm
Sundays	10.20am and every 14min until 1.34pm, then every 9min until 11.11pm

King's Heath via Balsall Heath-Hill Street

Weekdays	5.10am, 6.15, 6.30, then every 9min until 11.06pm
Sundays	9.45am, then every 14min until 1.00pm, then every 9min until 10.37pm

Hill Street-Moseley (STEAM)

Weekdays	5.56am, 6.26, 6.46, 7.08, 7.18, 7.27, 7.47, then every 9min until 11.39pm
Sundays	9.51am, then every 14min until 12.53pm, then every 9min until 10.42pm

Moseley-Hill Street

Weekdays	5.20am, 5.50, 6.10, 6.32, 6.42, 6.51, 7.11, then every 9min until 10.37pm
Sundays	9.51am, then every 14min until 12.53pm, then every 9min until 10.42pm

Albert Street-Nechells (HORSE)

Tues-Fri	6.30am, 6.58, 7.28, 7.43, then every 7min until 8.42pm, then every 8min until 11.30pm
Mon & Sat	6.30am, then every 7min until 11.32pm
Sundays	12.41pm, then every 7min until 10.57pm

Nechells-Albert Street

Tues-Fri	6.00am, 6.30, 7.00, 7.15, then every 7min until 8.26pm, then every 8min until 11.00pm
Mon & Sat	6.00am, then every 7min until 11.07pm
Sundays	12.15pm, then every 7min until 10.32pm

Colmore Row-New Inns (CABLE)

Weekdays	5.30am, 5.45, 6.00, 6.05, 6.10, 6.20, 6.30, 6.45, 7.04, then every 2min until 11.20pm
Sundays	9.35am, then every 4min until 2.35pm, then every 2min until 10.35pm

New Inns-Colmore Row

Weekdays	5.20am, 5.45, 6.00, 6.05, 6.10, 6.20, 6.30, 6.45, 7.00, 7.10, 7.15, 7.25, 7.32, then every 2min until 11.15pm
Sundays	9.37am, then every 4min until 2.40pm, then every 2min until 10.28pm

Old Square-Perry Barr (STEAM)

Weekdays	6.15am, 6.45, 7.19, 7.28, 7.37, then every 7min until 11.44pm
Sundays	10.14am, then every 13min until 1.42pm, then every 7min until 11.00pm

Perry Barr-Old Square

Weekdays	4.45am, 5.50, 6.20, 6.30, 6.40, 6.48, then every 7min until 11.17pm
Sundays	9.17am, then every 13min until 12.45pm, then every 7min to 10.35pm

Navigation Street-Pershore Road (Cotteridge) (ELECTRIC)

Weekdays	5.55am, 6.34, 6.50, then every 10min until 11.20pm
Sundays	10.36am, then every 13min until 2.10pm, then every 10min until 11.00pm

Pershore Road (Cotteridge)-Navigation Street

Weekdays	5.15am, 5.54, 6.10, then every 10min until 10.40pm
Sundays	9.56am, then every 13min until 1.30pm, then every 19min until 10.29pm

Old Square-Saltley (STEAM)

Weekdays	5.10am, 5.45, 6.15, 6.45, then frequently until 11.10pm
Sundays	9.40am, then every 13min until 1.08pm, then every 7min until 10.36pm

Saltley-Old Square

Weekdays	5.00am, 6.00, 6.30, 7.02, then frequently until 11.27pm
Sundays	9.57am, then every 13min until 1.25pm, then every 7min until 10.53pm

Station Street-Sparkbrook (STEAM)

Weekdays	5.30am, 5.40, 5.55, 6.10, 6.20, 6.30, 6.37, 6.45, 6.52, 7.00, 7.07, 7.15, 7.22, 7.28, then every 4/5min until 11.40pm
Sundays	10.15am, then every 10min until 2.05pm, then every 5min until 11.05pm

Sparkhill-Station Street

Weekdays	5.10am, 5.16, 5.31, 5.46, 5.56, 6.06, 6.13, 6.21, 6.28, 6.36, 6.43, 6.51, 6.58, 7.05, then every 4/5min until 11.16pm

College Road-Station Street

Weekdays	5.10am, 5.25, 5.40, 5.50, 6.00, 6.07, 6.15, 6.22, 6.30, 6.37, 6.45, 6.52, 7.00, then every 4/5min until 11.10pm
Sundays	9.45am, then every 10min until 2.04pm, then every 5min until 10.35pm

Station Street-Yardley (Swan) (ELECTRIC)

Weekdays	5.25am, then frequently until 11.38pm
Sundays	10.05am, then frequently until 11.21pm

Small Heath-Station Street

Weekdays	5.05am, then frequently until 11.18pm
Sundays	9.40am, then frequently until 11.01pm

Yardley (Swan)-Station Street

Weekdays	4.44am, then frequently until 11.08pm
Sundays	9.30am, then frequently until 10.51pm

Omnibuses

Note: All services are horse-drawn except where indicated

High Street-Acocks Green
(Spread Eagle) via Greet and Tyseley 3d

Weekdays	8.30am, then every 60min until 9.30pm; extra evening bus 9.40pm
Sundays	2.30pm, then every 60min until 8.30pm; extra evening bus 9.30pm

Acocks Green-High Street

Weekdays	8.30am, then every 60min until 9.30pm; extra evening bus 10.30pm
Sundays	2.30pm, then every 60min until 8.30pm; extra evening bus 9.30pm

Dale End-Alum Rock (Highfield Road) 2d

Weekdays	8.00am, then every 60min until 11.00pm
Sundays	3.00pm, then every 60min until 11.00pm

Alum Rock-Dale End

Weekdays	7.30am, then every 60min until 10.30pm
Sundays	2.30pm, then every 60min until 9.30pm

New Street Station-Balsall Heath (Mary Street) 1d

Weekdays	7.30am, then every 5min until 11.15pm
Sundays	1.20pm, then every 5min until 11.05pm

Balsall Heath-New Street Station

Weekdays	7.15am, then every 5min until 11.00pm
Sundays	1.40pm, then every 5min until 10.45pm

Albert Street-Bordesley Green 2d

Weekdays	8.00am, then every 30min until 11.00pm
Sundays	2.35pm, then every 30min until 10.05pm

Bordesley Green-Albert Street

Weekdays	7.30am, then every 30min until 10.30pm
Sundays	2.05pm, then every 30min until 9.35pm

Dale End-Castle Bromwich (Bradford Hotel) 6d

Weekends   9.00am, 10.00, 10.30, 11.00, 2.15pm, then
only   every 15min until 8.30pm

Castle Bromwich-Dale End

Weekends   11.30am, 12.00, 12.30pm, 3.30, then every
only   15min until 9.45pm

General Hospital-Five Ways 1d

Weekdays   8.20am, then every 10min until 10.50pm
Sundays   12.20pm, then every 10min until 10.30pm

Five Ways-General Hospital

Weekdays   8.00am, then every 10min until 10.30pm
Sundays   12.00 noon, then every 10min until 10.50pm

Albert Street-Green Lanes 2½d

Weekdays   7.25am, then every 20min until 11.05pm
Sundays   2.40pm, then every 20min until 10.30pm

Left: Open balcony tramcars Nos 377, 337, 152 and 340 blink in the sunlight as they peer out of the doorways at Witton Depot on 22 March 1939. Built by the Borough of Aston Manor the depot was taken over by the Corporation from 1 January 1912. *The Prince's Trust*

Green Lanes-Albert Street

Weekdays   7.25am, then every 20min until 11.05pm
Sundays   3.10pm, then every 20min until 10.50pm

New Street-Hagley Road (The Bear) 2d

Weekdays   9.04am, then every 15min until 10.54pm
Sundays   10.40am, then every 20min until 2.00pm, then
            every 15min until 10.55pm

Hagley Road-New Street

Weekdays   8.30am, then every 15min until 10.20pm
Sundays   10.05am, then every 20min until 1.25pm, then
            every 15min until 10.15pm

New Street-Hagley Road (King's Head)
(Motor 'Buses) 2d

Weekdays   7.43am, 7.58, 8.08, 8.18, 8.28, then every
            5min until 11.30pm
Sundays   10.25am, then every 5min until 10.45pm

Hagley Road-New Street

Weekdays   7.15am*, 7.30, 7.40*, 7.50, 8.00, then every
            5min until 11.00pm
Sundays   10.00am, then every 5min until 10.40pm
            * from the Bear Hotel

Hagley Road (Ivy Bush)-Handsworth Wood
(via Hockley & Monument Road) 4d

Weekdays   7.30am, then every 60min until 6.30pm (until
only   7.30pm on Saturdays only)

Handsworth Wood-Hagley Road

Weekdays   8.30am, then every 60min until 7.30pm
only

New Street-Harborne 3d

Weekdays   7.20am*, 7.30*, 7.40*, then every 8, 9, or
            10min until 11.06pm (until 11.20pm on
            Saturdays only)
Sundays   10.35am, then every 15min until 2.34pm, then
            every 8, 9, or 10min until 10.53pm
            *from Five Ways

Harborne-New Street

Weekdays   7.20am, then every 8, 9, or 10min until
            10.35pm; extra evening bus 10.40 (half fare
            between General Hospital and Post Office)
Sundays   10.00am, then every 15min until 2.00pm, then
            every 9/10min until 10.19pm

Albert Street-Ladypool Road
(corner of Brighton Road) 2d

Weekdays   8.08am, then every 15min until 11.08pm
Sundays   2.37pm, then every 15min until 11.08pm

Ladypool Road-Albert Street

Weekdays   7.37am, then every 15min until 10.37pm
Sundays   2.07pm, then every 15min until 10.37pm

New Street-Ladywood Road 1d

Weekdays   7.46am, then every 12min until 12 noon, then
            every 9/10min until 10.57pm
Sundays   2.07pm, then every 10min until 11.07pm

Ladywood Road-New Street

Weekdays 8.04am, then every 12min until 12.20pm, then every 9/10min until 11.17pm

Sundays 1.47pm, then every 10min until 10.47pm

Hockley Brook-Monument Road 2d

Weekdays 9.00am, then every 60min until 8.00pm; extra evening bus 9.00pm Saturdays only

Sundays 2.30pm, then every 60min until 9.30pm

Monument Road-Hockley Brook

Weekdays 8.30am, then every 60min until 7.30pm; extra evening bus 8.30pm Saturdays only

Sundays 2.00pm, then every 60min until 9.00pm

Dale End-Nechells 2d

Weekdays 8.25am, then every 30min until 3.25pm, then every 15min until 11.05pm

Sundays 12.55pm, then every 30min until 7.55pm, then every 15min until 11.25pm

Nechells-Dale End

Weekdays 6.50am, then every 30min until 2.50pm

Sundays 10.50am, then every 30min until 7.20pm

New Street-Quinton 5d

Weekdays only 9.10am

Bearwood-Quinton 3d

Weekdays 7.30am, then every 60min until 9.30pm

Sundays 9.30am, then 30min past the hour until 2.30pm, then every 30min until 9.30pm

Quinton-Bearwood

Weekdays 8.00am, then every 60min until 10.00pm

Sundays 10.00am, then every 60min until 3.00pm, then every 30min until 9.30pm

New Street-Ryland Street (Horsfalls) 1d

Weekdays 7.40am, then every 12min until 11.50am, then every 9/10min until 10.52pm

Sundays 2.10pm, then every 12min until 11.12pm

Ryland Street-New Street

Weekdays 7.58am, then every 12min until 12.10pm, then every 9/10min until 11.12pm

Sundays 1.52pm, then every 12min until 10.52pm

Yardley (Swan)-Sheldon (Wheatsheaf) 1d

Summer months only

High Street-Shirley 6d

Weekdays 9.00am, then every 60min until 9.00pm, then 10.00pm* and 11.00pm

Sundays 9.00am, 10.30, 2.30pm, then every 15min until 8.00pm, then 9.00pm

Saturdays only

Shirley-High Street

Weekdays 8.00am, then every 60min until 8.00pm, then 9.00pm†, 10.00pm†, 11.00pm*

Sundays 12.00 noon, 12.30pm, 2.00pm, 3.00pm, then every 15min until 10.00pm

†Sparkhill only; *Saturdays only*

Dale End-Washwood Heath 2d

Weekdays 8.35am, then every 30min until 10.35pm

Sundays 9.00am, 10.00, 10.30, 11.00, 2.15pm then every 15min until 8.30pm, then 9.05pm, 9.35, 10.05 and 10.35.

Washwood Heath-Dale End

Weekdays 8.05am, then every 30min until 10.05pm

Sundays 11.30am, 12.00, 12.30, 3.30pm then every 15min until 9.45pm.

Left: On 19 January 1935, 24 Daimler COG5s, with bodies by the Birmingham Railway & Carriage Works and Metropolitan-Cammell-Weymann, were lined up to announce the introduction of these vehicles to the press. This is about a quarter of them, with their eager crew on hand.
D. R. Harvey Collection

Appendix 2. Birmingham Corporation Transport Vehicles in Service to 3 September 1939

1. TRAMS

At the head of each entry the following information is given: fleet numbers, class name, body maker, electrical equipment supplier, year entering service. Details of the seating capacity of the vehicles follow the convention (upper saloon/lower saloon).

1-20 **'Original bogie' cars**
UEC Co/Dick, Kerr & Co 1904
Purchased to inaugurate the Corporation's tramway service in January 1904, these bogie double-deckers seated 56 (28/28). They were fitted with top covers (1904/5) and platform vestibules (1924-9), and were affectionately known as the 'old bogies'.

21-70 **'Brill' class UEC Co/Dick, Kerr & Co 1905**
Obtained in three batches, these four-wheel double-deckers seated 48 (26/22), and were all in service by June 1906. They were progressively fitted with top covers (from 1911 onwards), and with platform vestibules (1923-8). In 1924 cars 55-61, 63-4, and 68 were fitted with bow current collectors for use on the Lodge Road Route 32. Withdrawal of the cars began with the closure of the Bolton and Hagley Road routes in 1930; two cars were sold on to Dover Corporation, and four to Merthyr Tydfil.

71-220 **'Radial' class**
UEC Co/Dick, Kerr & Co 1906
Mounted on Mountain & Gibson radial trucks, these four-wheel double-deckers entered service from August 1906 to March 1907. They seated 52 (28/24) and were fitted with top covers from new and with platform vestibules progressively from 1923.

221-270 **'Brill' class UEC Co/Dick Kerr & Co 1906**
Sharing the same specification as cars 21-70, these entered service from March to May 1907.

271-300 **'Brill' class UEC Co/Dick, Kerr & Co 1908**
With the same specification as cars 21-70 and 221-270, these entered service from March to April 1908.

301-360 **'301' class'UEC Co/Dick, Kerr & Co 1911**
Four-wheel double-deckers, these cars entered service from April to June 1911. Seating 52 (28/24), they were fitted with both top covers and vestibules from new, Nos 342 and 347 receiving totally enclosed top covers, in January 1921 and July 1922, the only Corporation four-wheelers so fitted.

361-400 **'301' class UEC Co/Dick, Kerr & Co 1911**
Essentially an extension of the contract for Nos 301-360, these cars had platforms which were 3in longer. They entered service from November 1911 to February 1912. Five of the batch (Nos 361, 367, 368, 375 and 379) were converted to single-deckers in 1917, as part of the Corporation's experiment with such cars on the Cannon Hill, Hagley Road and Nechells routes. They were all converted back to double-deck form between April and July 1923.

401-450 **'401' class UEC Co/Dick, Kerr & Co 1912**
Initially considered as an extension to the '301' class contract, these cars were very similar in specification, seating 54 (30/24). They entered service from August 1912 to March 1913.

451-452 **ex-CBT 178, 180   CBT Co/Brush 1903**
Acquired in July 1911, these bogie double-deckers had been built at Kyotts Lake Road by CBT in 1903. They were the longest cars operated in Birmingham, and were converted to single-deckers between February and March 1917, emerging with a seating capacity of 34 and standing room for 17. Finally converted to Corporation double-deck standard in January 1926, they re-emerged with seating for 71 (37/34).

453-468 **ex-CBT 193-208 Brush/Brush 1904**
Acquired from CBT in January 1912, these four-wheeled cars were re-equipped between December 1919 and June 1924, and fitted with top covers and platform vestibules between October 1923 and July 1925, to resemble the Corporation open-balcony design. The cars seated 49 (27/22), but were under-powered, and their height restricted them to certain routes.

Also, by the late 1930s, they offered a poor level of passenger comfort. The cars were withdrawn progressively between July 1937 and April 1939.

469   ex-CBT 239 Brush/Brush 1904

Originally a BMT car, this four-wheeler was acquired by CBT in 1909 and passed to the Corporation in January 1912. It seated 48 (26/22) but was not fitted with a top cover or platform vestibules, and was withdrawn in January 1925.

470-472   ex-CBT 240-242 CBT Co/Brush 1904

Passing from CBT in January 1912, these four-wheeled cars were re-equipped between September 1922 and March 1924, and fitted with top covers and platform vestibules between April 1923 and July 1925, to resemble Corporation open balcony cars. They seated 49 (27/22), but, like Nos 453-468, were under-powered, height-restricted to certain routes, and offered a poor level of comfort. The cars were withdrawn between January and June 1938.

473-480   ex-CBT 181-188 Brush/Brush 1903

Built as bogie cars, when received from CBT in July 1911 they had been fitted with four-wheel trucks. Originally seating 55 (29/26), the bodies of Nos 473, 476, 477 and 479 were considered too poor to warrant improvement, and they were withdrawn from service in September 1924. The other four cars were re-equipped between October 1919 and January 1924, and fitted with top covers and platform vestibules between August and October 1925, when the seating capacity rose to 57 (31/26). Showing their age by 1938, they were withdrawn that May and June.

481-483   ex-CBT 212-214 CBT Co/Brush 1904

With bodies identical to Nos 453-468, these four-wheeled cars enjoyed a similar history. Re-equipped between October 1921 and January 1924, and fitted with top covers and platform vestibules between December 1923 and October 1924, they seated 49 (27/22). Considered an outdated design, cars 482 and 481 were withdrawn in May and June 1938, and No 483 in March 1939.

484-497   ex-CBT 220, 222-7, 229, 231, 233-4, 236-8 Brush/Brush 1904

Selected from 22 four-wheeled CBT cars built by Brush in 1904, these were re-equipped between July 1921 and September 1924 and fitted with top covers and platform vestibules between November 1923 and December 1924,

producing cars seating 49 (27/22). An exception was No 493, which was converted to permanent way car PW11 owing to the poor condition of its bodywork. Nos 484, 488, 489, 491, 494, 496 and 497 were withdrawn with the Stratford Road services in January 1937, with 495 following that February, 490 in May 1938, 487 in June 1938, 486 and 492 in March 1939, and 485 that April.

498-501   ex-CBT 246-7, 249, 251 Brush/Brush 1905

Acquired in 1912, and identical to Nos 484-497, No 498 was converted to permanent way car PW12 in October 1920, and the remainder re-equipped: No 500 in November 1919, 499 in December 1923, and 501 in July 1924; these were fitted with top covers and platform vestibules between December 1923 and July 1924, finally seating 49 (27/22). The abandonment of Stratford and Warwick Road services in 1937 allowed their withdrawal: No 499 in January 1937, 500 in February 1937 and 501 in June 1938.

502-508   ex-CBT 152, 154, 156, 158, 160, 162, 164 ERCW/Brush/BTH 1901

Selected from 15 CBT four-wheeled cars, with bodies by the Electric Railway & Tramway Carriage Works, these were acquired in July 1911. They seated 48 (26/22), but proved hard-riding in service, and were converted to other uses: No 503 to permanent way car PW4 in July 1913, 506 to PW5 in June 1914, 505 to PW8 in December 1920, 502 to PW7 from March 1921, 507 to PW9 August 1921, 508 to PW10 from November 1921. Only No 504 continued in passenger service, until January 1924.

509-511   ex-CBT 166, 168, 170 CBT Co/Brush/BTH 1901-3

Identical to Nos 502-508, except that their bodies were built by CBT, these were selected from a batch of six such CBT cars when acquired in July 1911. Also hard-riding, they were converted to other uses: No 509 to a single-deck trailer in October 1916, 510 to a water car in November 1916, and 509 on to PW9 in December 1928. Only No 511 remained in passenger service, until April 1922.

512-586   '512' class UEC Co/Dick, Kerr & Co 1913

Bogie double-deckers, these cars entered service between October 1913 and December 1914. With top covers and platform vestibules from new, they seated 62 (34/28), having their open balconies enclosed between 1926 and 1930.

587-636   **'587' class Brush/BTH 1920**
A modification of the prewar '512' class, with different body and equipment suppliers, these entered service from March 1920 to March 1921. They had their open balconies enclosed between 1929 and 1932.

637-661   **'637' class MRC&W/English Electric Co 1923**
Developed from, but similar to, the '587' class, these 63-seat (35/28) totally enclosed cars entered service from October 1923 to January 1924.

662-681   **'662' class Brush/English Electric Co 1924**
With similar bodies and identical electrical equipment, these 63-seat (35/28) totally enclosed cars entered service from March and April 1924.

682-701   **'662' class Brush/English Electric Co 1924**
An extension of the '662' class order, these cars entered service from December 1924 to February 1925.

702-731   **'702' class Brush/English Electric Co 1925**
Nearly identical to the '662' class, these cars seated 62 (35/27) and entered service from September 1925 to January 1926.

732-761   **'EMB Air Brake' Brush/English Electric Co 1926**
These 63-seat (35/28) totally enclosed cars were the first to be fitted with EMB Co air brakes from new. They entered service from September 1926 to March 1927.

762-811   **'EMB Air Brake' Brush/English Electric Co 1928**
Developed from the above cars, this second generation had improved equipment. They seated 62 (35/27) and were distinguished by double the number of window panels on the upper deck to the lower one, and by being fitted with bow collectors rather than trolley poles. They entered service from September 1928 to February 1929.

812-841   **'M&T Air Brake' Short Bros/English Electric 1928**
With bodies identical to the '762' class, these cars had Maley & Taunton bogies and air brakes. They entered service from November 1928 to April 1929.

842   **Short Bros/English Electric 1929**
The first of two experimental lightweight aluminium-bodied trams, car 842 seated 63 (36/27) and entered service in November 1929.

843   **Brush/GEC 1930**
Birmingham's last new tram was another lightweight-bodied one which seated 60 (33/27) and entered service in September 1930.

---

2. TROLLEYBUSES

At the head of each entry the following information is given: fleet numbers, body maker, chassis maker, year entering service, registration numbers. Details of the seating capacity of the vehicles follow the convention (upper saloon/lower saloon).

First Series

1-12   **Roe/Railless 1922 OK 4823-4834**
These were the first top-covered double-deck trolleybuses in the UK, seating 51 (25/26), and with open stairs. These solid-tyred vehicles were withdrawn progressively between 1930 and 1932 and replaced by the Leyland TB2 vehicles listed below.

13   **Hora/AEC 1923**
A little-known single-deck demonstration vehicle which ran in Birmingham between August and October 1923.

13   **English Electric/EMB 1924 OL 4636**
Clearly not superstitious, Birmingham Corporation had a second No 13 in its trolleybus fleet, this one being a 48 (28/20)-seat open-staired double-decker, which entered trial service in 1924, remaining until 1926.

14-16   **Short Bros/AEC 604 1926 ON 2825-2827**
Additional vehicles to the same design as Nos 1-12, these also had 51-seater (25/26) bodies. They entered service in 1926, and were withdrawn in 1932.

17   **Vickers/AEC 607 1926 ON 3261**
Similar in style to 14-16, this 52 (26/26)-seat double-decker was the first Corporation trolleybus to feature a foot-pedal control. It was withdrawn in 1932.

18   **Guy/Guy BTX 1930 UK 8341**
As the original trolleybus fleet came due for replacement, several vehicles were evaluated. This Guy trolleybus had a six-wheeled chassis and enclosed stairs, seating 53 (27/26). It was classed as a demonstration vehicle and entered service on 26 February 1930, being used until 31 July 1931.

19   Guy/Guy RTX 1931 OG 9886

A second Guy six-wheeled demonstrator was obtained in 1931, and was run from 10 April, but it was returned to the manufacturer a week later, on 17 April, before entering regular service.

19   Leyland/Leyland FA3B 1931 OV 1175

Taking the fleet number of the returned Guy, this Leyland demonstrator seated 48 and entered service on 20 May 1931, remaining in service until 18 August 1931.

20   Guy/Guy BT 1931 OV 1194

This third Guy demonstrator, also obtained in 1931, which seated 48, also entered service on 20 May 1931 and ran until 27 May 1931.

Second Series

1-11   Short Bros/Leyland TB2 1932 OV 4001-4011

Taking the fleet numbers of most of the original trolleybuses, withdrawn in 1932, these Leyland four-wheelers seated 48 (27/21).

12-16   Brush/AEC 663T 1932 OJ 1012-1016

Also taking the fleet numbers of withdrawn vehicles, these AEC six-wheelers seated 58 (33/25).

17   Leyland/Leyland 1933 TJ 939

A Leyland six-wheeled demonstrator which seated 60 (32/28) and ran in service from 11 March to July 1933. It later returned on 9 July 1936 as No 68.

17-66   Metro-Cammell/Leyland TTBD2 1934 OC 1117-1166

These 50 six-wheeled Leyland vehicles seated 58 (33/25).

67   Metro-Cammell/Sunbeam MS2 1934 OC 6567

A six-wheeled Sunbeam demonstrator which seated 59 (31/28) and ran in Birmingham from 9 February to 24 March 1934.

68   Leyland/Leyland 1936 TJ 939

A Leyland six-wheeled demonstrator, formerly No 17, which seated 60 (32/28) and ran in service between 9 July 1936 and 1 October 1937.

Left: Tramcar No 50 was one of the second batch of cars, bought by the Corporation in 1905. Originally open top, by the early 1930s, when this shot was taken, it had been extensively upgraded, and eventually gave 42 years' service to the Corporation, being withdrawn in April 1947..*IAL*

Right: The interior of tramcar No 388, which entered service at the end of 1911. Originally fitted with longitudinal wooden seats, these were replaced with tilting transverse seats early in 1929, as shown here. They gave passengers 20 years of improved comfort before the car was withdrawn in December 1949. *Modern Transport/IAL*

67-78   **Metro-Cammell/Leyland TB5**
1937 COX 67-78
Four-wheeled Leyland vehicles which seated
53 (29/24).

79-90   **Metro-Cammell/Leyland TB7**
1940 FOK 79-90
A further 12 Leyland vehicles which seated 54
(30/24).

---

3. BUSES

At the head of each entry the following information is given:
fleet numbers, body maker, chassis maker, year entering
service, registration numbers. Details of the seating
capacity of the vehicles follows the convention (upper
saloon/lower saloon).

1-10   **LGOC/Daimler 1913 OA 1601-1610**
Birmingham Corporation's first motor
omnibuses were based on a Daimler chassis,
with a 40hp engine, fitted with a London
General Omnibus Co style body which seated
34 (18/16). The chassis were commandeered by
the War Department in 1914, and the bodies,
plus the vehicle registrations, were reused on
new chassis in 1915.

0-12   **Brush/Tilling-Stevens TTA1**
1914 O 8200-8212

13-29   **Brush/Tilling-Stevens TTA2**
1914 O 9913-9929

30   **Allen/Tilling-Stevens TS3**
1914 OA 5711
These vehicles were acquired from the BMMO
when the Corporation took over its services in
October 1914. They had been bought new in
1912 (No 30 in 1913) and were fitted with 34
(18/16)-seater bodies. Withdrawals began in
1916 with Nos 0-6, and continued until 1926
with No 30. The chassis from all but Nos 7, 8,
20 and 30 were used as the basis for
Corporation service vehicles.

31-40   **LGOC/Tilling-Stevens TS3**
1915 OA1601-1610
The bodies from the original Daimlers of 1913
were put on new Tilling-Stevens chassis,
producing vehicles with the same seating
capacity of 34 (18/16) and registration
numbers. In 1922 Nos 31-38 received bodies
from the Daimlers in the next batch of
omnibuses acquired, but all 10 vehicles were
withdrawn in 1926, Nos 38 and 39 becoming
service vehicles Nos 4 and 2.

41-49   **Dodson/Daimler Y 1916 OB 1596-1574**
                                   OB 2101-2103
50-52   **Brush/Daimler Y 1916 OB 2104-2106**

53-58   **Brush/Tilling-Stevens TS3**
1916 OB 2107-2112
Intended as a single batch of Daimler vehicles,
the chassis for Nos 53-58 were commandeered
by the War Ministry before the bodies, which
were from the ex-BMMO omnibuses 0-6, could
be fitted. In their place, Tilling-Stevens TS3
chassis were used. The Dodson bodies on Nos
41-49 seated 33 (18/15), whilst those on Nos
50-58 seated 34 (18/16). Withdrawals took
place over four years: 1924 (56), 1926 (53, 55),
1927 (41-52) and 1928 (54, 57, 58).

59   **Fry/AEC 503 1922 OK 3980**
The Corporation's first all-new postwar
omnibus boasted a seating capacity of 54
(28/26) and was bought after one month on
demonstration. It was withdrawn in 1927.

60-71   **Brush/AEC 503 1923 OK 8002-8013**
Similar to No 59, these 11 AECs had Brush
bodies which also seated 54 (28/26). No 62
was fitted with an experimental top cover in
1924, but did not run with this in public
service. Withdrawals began with 60 and 61
in 1927, and ended with 71, renumbered 471,
in 1930.

1-8   **Buckingham/Leyland A1**
1922 OK 5484-5491 (72-79)
These eight 20-seat single-deckers, with bodies
by local firm John Buckingham Ltd, were
acquired to work new outer suburban services
by one-man-operation. They were renumbered
72-79 in 1923, and reseated to 19-seaters in
1925, Nos 72, 74, 75 and 77 being renumbered
by having 400 added to their fleet number in
1930, and again by becoming 32, 34, 35 and
37 in 1931, the year they were withdrawn.
The other four vehicles had been withdrawn
in 1929.

80   **Buckingham/Daimler CK2**
1923 OK 9852
John Buckingham Ltd was also favoured for
the body on this 21-seat Daimler single-decker.
It was reseated to a 19-seater in 1925, and
renumbered 480 in 1930 and 38 in 1931, the
year of its withdrawal.

81-88   **Strachan & Brown/Daimler CK2**
1923 OL 1714-1721
Originally seating 24, the capacity of these
single-deckers was reduced by one in 1925.
Nos 82-4 and 86-9 were withdrawn in 1930,
Nos 81 and 85 being renumbered 39 and 40 the
same year, and withdrawn in 1931.

89-90   **Brush/AEC 503 1923 OK 8014-8015**
Similar to Nos 60-71, No 90 was withdrawn in 1929, followed by No 89 in 1931.

91-100   These fleet numbers were not allocated to new omnibuses in sequence, being held in reserve for various demonstrator vehicles.

101   **Brush/AEC 504 1924 OL 8100**
Birmingham's first top-covered omnibus seated 50 (26/24) and remained in service until 1935.

102-131   **Short Bros/AEC 504 1924 OM 201-230**
132-161   **Short Bros/AEC 504 1925 OM 9546-9575**
162-171   **Short Bros/AEC 504 1925 ON 1313-1322**
Delivered in three batches, these double-deckers seated 52 (26/26) and were fitted with top-covers from new. They gave between 10 and 13 years' service to the Corporation, being withdrawn progressively between 1934 and 1937.

29   **Brush/AEC 504 1926 ON 5400**
Allocated the fleet number of a Tilling-Stevens double-decker withdrawn in 1924, this 25-seater single-decker became an Instructional vehicle in April 1929.

172-191   **Short Bros/AEC 504 1926 OP 201-220**
192-201   **Thompson/AEC 504 1926 OP 221-230**
202-207   **Buckingham/AEC 504 1926 OP 231-236**
Despite having bodies by three different makers, these double-deckers all seated 52 (26/26) and were similar to Nos 102-171 of 1925. They were withdrawn progressively between 1934 and 1937.

208   **Short Bros/Guy BKX 1926 OP 237**
Birmingham Corporation's first six-wheeled omnibus seated 58 (32/26) and had a Daimler engine. It was fitted with a new chassis by Guy in 1927, and was withdrawn late in 1933.

209   **Short Bros/Karrier DD6 1927 OP 238**
Six-wheeler number two had an increased seating capacity of 60 (32/28) but a short service life, being withdrawn in 1929 and converted to service vehicle No 15, which it served as until 1938.

210-219   **Buckingham/AEC 507 1927 OP 3650-3659**
220-234   **Short Bros/ADC 507 1927 OP 7863-7877**
235-244   **Short Bros/ADC 507 1927 OX 1501-1510**
245-259   **Short Bros/ADC 507 1927 OX 1511-1525**
260-274   **Buckingham/ADC 507 1927 OX 1536-1550**

275-284   **Vickers/ADC 507 1927 OX 1526-1535**
285   **Short Bros/ADC 507 1927 OX 1570**
286-295   **Short Bros/ADC 507 1928 VP 1150-1159**
296-337   **Short Bros/ADC 507 1928/9 VP 1160-1201**
Although carrying the handywork of four different body makers, these vehicles were essentially variations upon the same design of double-decker. The change of chassis from AEC to ADC reflected a short-lived partnership between AEC and Daimler, which was known as Associated Daimler. All of the omnibuses were 52 (26/26)-seaters, except Nos 220-244 and 286-295, which were low-height vehicles with special knife-board individual seating on the top deck, arranged in a herringbone pattern; they seated 46 (20/26). Other exceptions were Nos 285 and 296-337, which seated 50 (24/26), the latter bodies also being metal-framed. These vehicles enjoyed relatively short working lives with the Corporation, being withdrawn progressively between 1933 and 1937.

99   **Leyland/Leyland TD1 1929 OF 3959**
Between January and September 1929 this omnibus carried the 52-seat (26/26) body from No 159, before being fitted with its intended one. The vehicle was fitted with an oil (diesel) engine and purchased by the Corporation in July 1932.

51-60   **Guy/Guy Conquest 1929 OF 3960-3969**
61-80   **Guy/Guy Conquest 1930 OF 6071-6090**
Taking the fleet numbers of withdrawn vehicles, these Guy single-deckers seated 25. They were withdrawn progressively between 1934 and 1938.

338-367   **Brush/AEC Regent 1929 OF 3970-3999**
Delivered on into early 1930, these Regents seated 50 (26/24), with the following remaining in service on 3 September 1939: 340-3, 345-7, 349-50, 352-4, 356 and 358-67.

209   **Metro-Cammell/AEC Regent 1930 OG 209**
338-339   **Bush/AEC Regent 1930 OG 3638-3639**
368   **Short Bros/AEC Regent 1930 OF 8368**
Four vehicles, mostly out of sequence, being the first all-metal-bodied bus (209); two replacements for older vehicles (338-9) and an ex-demonstration model (368). All but 339, withdrawn in 1938, worked on after 3 September 1939.

Above: In the late 1920s, 75 of the 150 'Radial' class tramcars (Nos 71-220) had their interiors modernised, with improved padded seating. This view of No 134, which entered service late in 1906, shows detail of the lining out on the dash. The car was withdrawn in November 1938. *IAL*

369-408   **English Electric/AEC Regent 1930**
OG 369-408
409-443   **Vulcan/AEC Regent 1930 OG 409-443**
These Regents had bodies supplied by two makers, 369-407 being 48-seaters (27/21) by English Electric, and 409-443 to the same configuration by Vulcan. No 408 had a 47-seater (26/21) English Electric body. On 3 September 1939 the following remained in service: 369, 371, 373-81, 383-5, 387, 389, 391-404, 411-2, 418, 420-1, 423-5, 428-31, 433-6, 438, 440 and 443.

81-90   **Metro-Cammell/Morris Dictator 1931**
OV 4081-4090
These 10 Morris Dictator single-deckers seated 34.

444-483   **Short Bros/AEC Regent 1931**
OV 4444-4483
484-503   **Metro-Cammell/AEC Regent 1931**
OV 4484-4503
A batch of Regent double-deckers, which seated 48 (27/21). Nos 444-483 had bodies by Short Bros, the remainder being by Metro-Cammell. Only No 455 had been withdrawn by 3 September 1939.

47-50   **Metro-Cammell/Morris Dictator 1933**
OJ 9347-9350
These four Morris Dictator single-deckers had 34-seater bodies, and were renumbered 77-80 in 1935.

504   **Brush/Morris Imperial 1933**
OC 504
505   **English Electric/Morris Imperial 1933**
OC 505
Two double-deckers with different bodies: 504 had a 51-seat (29/22) one by Brush, and 505, a 47-seat one by English Electric.

507-553   **Metro-Cammell/Morris Imperial 1933**
OC 507-553
A batch of Morris Imperial double-deckers with 50-seater (28/22) bodies. Nos 519-20, 532, 536 and 553 were withdrawn in 1939.

554-563   **BRCW/Daimler CP6 1933 OC 554-563**
Ten Daimler CP6 double-deckers with 51-seater (29/22) bodies.

208   **Metro-Cammell/Guy Arab 6LW 1934**
OC 8208
A rebuilt demonstration model double-decker; by 1935 it had been fitted with a 54-seat (30/24) body.

564-578   **BRCW/Daimler COG5 1934**
AOB 564-578
The first of many orders for Daimler COG5 double-deckers, these with 48-seater (26/22) bodies.

579-633   **Metro-Cammell/Daimler COG5 1934**
AOB 579-633
A similar batch to the above, with Metro-Cammell bodies.

634-673   **BRCW/Daimler COG5 1935**
AOG 634-673
674-688   **Northern Counties/Daimler COG5 1935**
AOG 674-688

689-693 **Short Bros/Daimler COG5 1935**
AOG 689-693
A further batch of 60 COG5 double-deckers, with 48-seat (26/22) bodies supplied by three makers.

694-743 **Metro-Cammell/Daimler COG5 1935**
AOP 694-743
744-793 **BRCW/Daimler COG5 1935**
AOP 744-793
One hundred COG5 double-deckers, with a split body order: 694-743 had 48-seater (26/22) bodies by Metro-Cammell, 744-784 similar ones by the BRCW, whilst 785-793 had 54-seater (30/24) bodies by the same maker.

42-61 **Metro-Cammell/Daimler COG5/40 1935**
AOP 42-61
62-76 **Strachens/Daimler COG5/40 1935**
AOP 62-76
Single-deck COG5s fitted with 34-seater bodies from two makers

93 **Park Royal/AEC Q 1935 AHX 63**
A former demonstrator, this double-decker was acquired in November 1935 and reseated to a 56-seater (29/27) in 1936.

32-41 **Metro-Cammell/Daimler COG5/40 1936**
BOL 32-41
Ten single-deck versions of the COG5, which were used as ambulances during the war.

94 **Metro-Cammell/Daimler COG5 1936**
BOP 94
A 52-seater (28/24) double-deck demonstrator purchased in December 1936.

794-843 **BRCW/Daimler COG5 1936**
BOP 794-843
844-893 **Metro-Cammell/Daimler COG5**
1936 BOP 844-893
Another 100 COG5s, with 54-seat (30/24) bodies.

894-963 **Metro-Cammell/Daimler COG5 1937**
COH 894-963
A batch of 70 COG5s with 54-seat (30/24) bodies.

964-968 **Leyland/Leyland TD4c 1937 COX 964-968**
Five all-Leyland double-deckers with 52-seater (28/24) bodies.

969-999 **Metro-Cammell/Daimler COG5 1937**
COX 969-999
An extra 31 COG5s with 54-seat (30/24) bodies.

1000-1033 **Metro-Cammell/Daimler COG5 1937**
CVP 100-133
A further 34 COG5s with 54-seat (30/24) bodies.

1034-1038 **Metro-Cammell/AEC Regent 1937**
CVP 134-138
Five more Regents with 54-seat (30/24) bodies.

1039-1138 **Metro-Cammell/Daimler COG5 1937**
CVP 139-238
A batch of 100 COG5s with 54-seat (30/24) bodies.

1139 **Metro-Cammell/Daimler COG5 1937**
DON 439
A demonstrator on hire from March 1937, this had a 54-seat (30/24) body.

102-150 **Metro-Cammell/Daimler COG5 1938**
EOG 102-150
151-200 **BRCW/Daimler COG5 1938**
EOG 151-200
Another 99 COG5s, with 102-50 having 54-seat (30/24) bodies by Metro-Cammell, and 151-200 similar bodies by the BRCW.

211-295 **Metro-Cammell/Leyland TD6c 1939**
EOG 211-295
A large order for 85 Leylands, with 52-seater (28/24) bodies.

1140-1235 **Metro-Cammell/Daimler COG5 1939**
FOF 140-235
A further 96 COG5s with 54-seat (30/24) bodies.

1236 **Metro-Cammell/Daimler COG5 1939**
FOF 236
1237 **English Electric/Daimler COG5 1939**
FOF 237
1238 **Park Royal/Daimler COG5 1939**
FOF 238
1239 **Brush/Daimler COG5 1939**
FOF 239
1240-1269 **BRCW/Daimler COG5 1939**
FOF 240-269
A final 34 COG5s fitted with 54-seat (30/24) bodies from a variety of builders.

Information on vehicles entering service with Birmingham Corporation Transport after 3 September 1939 can be found in the companion volume to this book *Birmingham Corporation Transport 1939-1969.*

Acknowledgements

Birmingham Corporation Transport 1939-1969

I am very grateful to the following individuals and organisations, without whose help this book would not have been possible: the Staff at Birmingham Reference Library, June Collins, Ray Cresswell and Brierley Office Products, Louise Hampson, Mellanie Hartland, David Harvey, the library of the Ironbridge Gorge Museum Trust, Malcolm Keeley, Alan Mills and members of the Omnibus Society, the National Motor Museum, and Ron Thomas. I am also grateful to G. H. F. Atkins for the loan of his photographs, and to the following photographers for being there at the right time: Lance Brown, W. A. Camwell, R. T. Coxon, W. J. Haynes, A. D. Packer, R. B. Parr and H. B. Priestley.

I also wish to give special thanks to Nick Grant and Peter Waller at Ian Allan Publishing Ltd for their patience and forbearance, and to Winston Bond, Rosie Thacker and Glyn Wilton of the National Tramway Museum for all of their help and support with this project.

Paul Collins MSc, MSocSc, PhD
Wollaston, Stourbridge, West Midlands

As stated, these volumes are not intended to be vehicle-based histories. Nonetheless, since the publication in 1999 of *Birmingham Corporation Transport 1939-1969*, some readers have been kind enough to point out detailed corrections to, or provide additional information for, the following captions. I am grateful to those who took the time and trouble to contact the publishers:

p.25 *Below*
Guy Arab II 5LW No 1401 became a dual-control trainer numbered 23 and received the wartime Brush body from a rebodied AEC Regent.

p.34 *Above*
The tarmac the bus was standing on 'patched *the* road after the removal of the tram lines 10 years earlier.'

p.35 *Left*
Leyland only built two PD2 *prototypes.*

p.36 *Above*
No 1732 was a PD2/1, not a PD2/2 as stated.

p.40 *Above right*
Daimler COG5 No 1239 of 1939 had a one-off Brush body.

p.48 *Right*
Daimler COG5 No 57 was running light when photographed on 28 June 1949, not working the 24 service to Warstock, hence the destination being part wound-down.

p.76 *Below right*
Daimler CVG6 No 2880 was fitted with a Manchester-style front in the late 1950s as an experiment.

p.80 *Left*
The bus waiting on tram replacement service 64 on 4 July 1953 was probably No 3023, not No 3203, which was not introduced until the following year.

p.94 *Above*
At the time it was photographed the Guy Arab II 5LW of 1945 was driver trainer vehicle No 93.

p.107 *Left*
Only 10 of the batch of Daimler Fleetlines delivered in 1964 had experimental windscreens.